Embrace The Journey

Balance Purpose and Progress

A journey of goals, growth and grace

By Jenny Carlson

Grace &
Growth
PRESS

Published by Grace & Growth Press

ISBN: 979-8-218-77375-5

Cover design by the author

Interior layout by the author

Printed in the United States of America

For more information: embrace-the-journey.org

Dedication

To Memaw (Bruenhilde Wegmann),

who showed me what it was to have an unstoppable spirit
and for whom hope and beauty were always in view. I carry
you with me every day.

To Wanda Robertson –

Sunshine and firecrackers, who loved fiercely, and who
showed me the way home. I love you to the moon and back.

My heart awaits the day we will be reunited.

And—

For every soul who dares to grow—
To those who keep walking when the path is uncertain—
For anyone who has stood in the storm—
To the weary, the hopeful, and the brave—

As you rebuild, realign, and rise again...
You are proof the journey is never wasted.

Gratitude/Acknowledgements

For my "Mom," Marge VanDoren—

for loving me by choice. I learned to have grit and keep going from you.

For Karey Messina—

for reinforcing "this is a book" even as I fought against it. The Spirit spoke and you confirmed it.

For Debbie Dunn—

mentor and sister in Christ, dear friend, a faithful cheerleader. You helped make this book better, and I thank you.

For Debra Stahl—

Your unending love and encouragement in all that I pursue.

To Holly Blackwood—

for your friendship and generosity. Your insight and thoughtful feedback helped shape this work into its best form.

To Kevin and Margaret Brown—

for walking alongside me with vision, seeing not just what was, but what could be. You challenge me to look deeper, think beyond the surface, and align. You are truly treasured.

To all who have walked this journey with me—

personally and professionally— Your words, your presence, your support made a difference.

And to those who created roadblocks,

who minimized or dismissed me, or caused me pain — thank you, too. Without resistance, there would be no refinement.

It is in the overcoming that we find our greatest victories.

Table of Contents

Introduction..1

    What to Expect..4

    Getting Started..6

Waypoint One: The Destination 6

    Defining Your Core Values...9

    Reframing Success..13

    Your Inherent Value 14

    Goal Manager, Goal Keeper, Goal Seeker 16

    Finding Joy in the Process 19

Waypoint Two: Goal Stoppers – Overcoming Obstacles...................20

    Enthusiasm vs. Passion..20

    Common Goal Stoppers 21

Waypoint Three: Planning the Journey 30

    Lay of the Land..30

    Trip Plan 35

    Anchors 37

    Letting Go Without Regret 42

    Navigating Rough Waters...43

    Planning For Storms 54

    Budget: Planning The Resources 61

    Travel Partners 67

    Protecting Your Focus & Boundaries...................................78

Table of Contents (continued)

Waypoint Four: Moving Forward: Journey Systems 83

Building Your Transportation System....................................86

Creating Rest & Renewal Spaces....................................89

Choosing the Right Activities..94

Saying "Yes" and "No" Wisely 96

Automating & Streamlining Your Obligations 99

Minimizing Risk 105

Waypoint Five: Packing for Success 110

Backpack/Suitcase..110

Sustenance/Fuel...111

Map 113

Compass 114

Emergency Beacon..115

Part Two: Embrace the Journey – Turning Goals Into Action 118

Basics of Goal Setting 118

Understanding & Using Your Workstyle 122

Embrace Your Unique Blend 127

Reflection, Action, and Moving Forward 138

Bonus: Top Tips for the Road 140

Author's Note 147

About the Author 148

Introduction

Life is a journey. It is filled with experiences, growth, memories, and relationships. Our journeys often contain glorious moments of victory mixed with challenges or setbacks. Along the way, we discover passions and interests that inspire us to dream. Yet our hearts desire more—to stretch beyond the limits we perceive. We are wired to seek purpose, meaning, and accomplishment, even as we navigate the ebb and flow of daily life. Yet, the road is rarely straight. Confusion, hesitation, and a lack of focus can cloud our path. So how do we respond to these twists and turns? We embrace them.

In today's world, success is often portrayed as public and measurable: likes, shares, followers, awards. This emphasis on visible accomplishments sometimes diminishes the quiet and internal victories that truly shape our lives. Rarely do we celebrate the process—the journey—as much as we do the destination. But here's the truth: **the journey is as valuable, if not more so, than the goal itself.** When we "Embrace the Journey," we honor every step—the ups and downs, the lessons learned, and the moments of growth that lead us to our desired destination.

No goal is too small, no dream too bold. All goals have value. Unfortunately, our world often devalues personal milestones that lack public recognition. But whether your goal is professional success, personal growth, or improving your daily habits, it has inherent worth. Your purpose, fulfillment, and acts of service for others may not always garner applause, but they remain deeply significant.

Before we dive into this book, let's take a moment to align our mindset. Every goal has value—because every person is divinely unique. Our desires, our passions, our choices—they all reflect that uniqueness. Embracing who we are, and truly owning it, is the first step to uncovering the joy and purpose waiting along our journey.

The truth of ourselves—the truth we're willing to see—can launch us past the goal stoppers, the hangups, the insecurities that have chained us for too long. This path will ask us to find a balance: to take in expert advice, to gain new knowledge, but also to release the weight of what others think of us. That weight holds us back.

So, be the Phoenix. Break free. Soar. Be wonderfully and uniquely magnificent.

Every choice comes with trade-offs. But when we fully accept both the positives and the negatives, we are set free—free to focus on what truly matters.

There will be moments when we're torn between two choices, trying to navigate the "shoulds" while tuning into where our values actually want to lead us. That can be a real struggle. A stay-at-home parent, for example, may deeply treasure extra time with their children, even while wrestling with financial limitations or the weight of societal judgment. A working parent may feel deeply fulfilled by their career, yet carry guilt and regret about the time spent away from family.

Neither choice is inherently better. Each is a "mixed bag" of joy and challenge. But recognizing this truth allows us to loosen the grip of guilt and instead embrace the full picture—appreciating every facet of the life we're choosing.

In much the same way, when others criticize our decisions, it's because they can't see the vision or values we hold dear. And while their judgment may cause us to shrink at times, the "untwisted truth" is this: their perspective does not diminish the worth of our goals, nor the reasons behind them.

Embracing the journey means finding peace in our choices—and walking forward without hesitation, without apology.

This book is here to guide you on that very journey—to help you set meaningful goals, embrace the process, and overcome the obstacles along the way.

What to Expect

This book is divided into two sections:

Section 1: The Journey

This section explores the emotional and mental aspects of goal-setting and personal growth. Together, we'll address common roadblocks like self-limiting beliefs, the fear of failure, and the tendency to dismiss the "in-between" moments. You'll learn how to embrace the full scope of your journey, from the mundane to the miraculous. We'll celebrate the value of every step and uncover the strategies that transform obstacles into opportunities for growth.

Section 2: The Framework

This section is packed with practical tools, routines, and strategies to help you achieve your goals while maintaining balance. Topics include:

- **Goal Setting Basics**: Defining your goals, using the SMART method, breaking them down, prioritizing, setting deadlines, and tracking progress.

- **Actionable Tasks and Routines**: Decluttering, task prioritization, habit-stacking, time-blocking, productivity techniques, weekly and monthly planning, using tools and systems, and building accountability.

- **Self-Awareness**: Understanding your unique strengths, weaknesses, and work style, and aligning them with strategies that resonate with you.

- **Adapting to What Resonates**: Whether you're structured, flexible, detail-oriented, or a big-picture thinker, you'll find approaches tailored to your style.

- **Avoiding Burnout**: Setting realistic timelines, celebrating small wins, and integrating self-care into your journey.

- **Quizzes and Action Plans**: These exercises will help you better understand your work style, adapt your tactics, and create a personalized roadmap to success.

A Workbook for Your Journey

This book also serves as a workbook with exercises designed to help you:

- Discover your strengths and weaknesses.

- Tailor goal-setting tactics to your needs.

- Break down goals into actionable steps using the SMART framework.

- Create routines that align with your aspirations and lifestyle.

You can choose to read through the book sequentially or jump straight into the activities. Whether you're someone who loves planning every detail or someone who thrives on flexibility, this book is designed to meet you where you are.

If you're reading this, chances are you have a goal in mind or are searching for clarity and purpose. The good news? Your goals are within reach. Together, we will uncover the path to your success, step by step. Decide here and now to commit to embracing the journey—your journey—to success.

Your journey starts here!

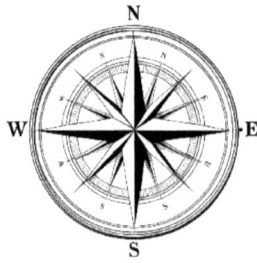

Getting Started

Planning and embarking on a journey is thrilling. Often, we spend months organizing the details, researching activities, and booking accommodations. The prospect of what lies ahead ignites our imagination and builds anticipation. Thoughtful preparation includes leaving space for spontaneous moments or well-earned rest, ensuring a comprehensive and enjoyable experience.

Whether you're seasoned in goal-setting and navigating your way to each destination or new to the process, this book can elevate your experience and keep you aligned with your aspirations. For those who love planners, or the hand-written record, The *Embrace the Journey Planner* is available to be your companion on this adventure, offering a practical tool to stay on track.

As you envision, plan, and chart your course, prepare to embrace every aspect of the journey. Use the tools and strategies that resonate with you, and tailor them to your unique path.

The Destination

The concept of a destination is multifaceted. Goals often seem straightforward initially, but they can carry deeper layers of meaning. You may already know the goal you want to achieve, feeling focused and ready to begin. If you're accomplished in certain areas, you might even choose to skip ahead, prioritizing time savings over revisiting familiar territory. However, it's worth reflecting on your "destination" and its source to ensure alignment with your deeper purpose.

Sometimes, we strive toward personal or career milestones only to find they don't fulfill us as expected. If you're ready to move forward, consider reading the next section, *The Destination – Source*, before advancing to the rest of the journey.

The Destination – Source

One significant influence on our choice of destinations is our moral values—those principles that shape what we deem important in life. Values help us uncover our "why" - the core purpose that drives us. Our most fulfilling destinations are deeply rooted in this purpose.

Values are neither inherently "good" nor "bad," but they reveal our priorities and where we choose to spend our time. Often, there's a gap between the values we express and those we live.

You will hear me use the term **"untwisted truth"** throughout this book. It's the deeper truth—the truth without qualification points. Often raw, and sometimes painful, it is the most useful and powerful version of **truth**.

The untwisted truth here is that how we spend our time reflects either our true values or **what we are willing to risk**.

Every choice we make comes with a trade-off. When we invest time and energy into one area of life, we naturally divert it from another. If we say we value faith, family, or personal growth but consistently prioritize work, social obligations, or distractions instead, we must ask ourselves: **What are we risking?** Are we willing to risk the depth of our relationships, our well-being, or our sense of purpose?

Sometimes, we risk things intentionally—we accept short-term sacrifices for long-term gains. Other times, the risk is unintentional, a slow drift away from what we claim to hold dear. Either way, recognizing this dynamic gives us the power to adjust our course.

When we notice a misalignment between our stated and lived values, we have the power to realign them. This can happen in three ways:

1. **Changing our efforts to focus on our stated values.** This means making conscious decisions to prioritize what we say matters to us the most.

2. **Acknowledging our current priorities, leading to an honest declaration of what we truly value.** Instead of living in conflict, we accept that our actions reveal our true values and adjust accordingly.

3. **Recognizing why fear—or our goal itself—is not a priority in our actions, and why something else takes precedence.** Sometimes, we aren't pursuing what we say we want because fear, uncertainty, or self-doubt is holding us back. Other times, we realize that the goal isn't truly ours—it's an expectation we've adopted. Understanding these barriers allows us to either recommit with clarity or release the goal without guilt.

Each of these paths creates harmony, reducing obstacles to achieving our goals and ensuring that what we treasure most is not lost to what simply demands our attention.

Defining Your Core Values

If you've never taken the time to define your values, now is a perfect moment to reflect and evaluate where you stand. This exercise requires absolute self-honesty and introspection.

Start by creating **two lists**:

1. **Stated Values**: These are the values you believe you hold and want to prioritize. Write these down as they come to mind—your initial gut reaction is a great starting point. What you want, or could even say "ache" for.

2. **Exhibited Values**: This list may take more time and introspection. Think about where you spend your time and energy. Your actions—how you live day-to-day—reveal your true priorities.

Compare the two lists. Are your stated and exhibited values aligned, or are there discrepancies? Don't worry if they aren't a perfect match—this process is about awareness and creating alignment.

Use the list of values below as a starting point, but don't feel limited by it. If a value that deeply resonates with you isn't included, make sure to add it. This exercise is about discovering what truly matters to **you**—not what you think *should* matter.

As you go through the list, pay close attention to your gut reaction—that split second before logic, reasoning, or external influences take over. That moment holds an important clue about what speaks to your core. Try to set aside any preconceived notions about who you think you are or who you believe you *should* be. Instead, focus on what stirs something within you.

This is your opportunity to identify the values that feel most **authentic** to you. Let go of expectations, release self-judgment, and trust what resonates at your deepest level.

Values to Consider

Compassion	Intelligence
Kindness	Happiness
Sincerity	Authenticity
Growth	Honesty
Love	Education
Peace	Influence
Understanding	Service
Community	Friendship
Beauty	Harmony
Balance	Stability
Security	Independence
Achievement	Faith
Adventure	Knowledge
Justice	Trust
Curiosity	Freedom
Reputation	Simplicity
Health	Leadership
Success	Relevance
Fun	Creativity
Responsibility	Benevolence
Courage	Loyalty

Status	Optimism
Perfection	Determination
Spontaneity	Pleasure
Purpose	Integrity
Power	Competency
Dependability	Recognition
Wealth	

Reflection Exercise

Take a few minutes to review your chosen destination or goal, if you've already identified one. Ask yourself:

1. Does my destination align with my core values?

2. How do my stated and exhibited values support or contradict this destination?

Write your thoughts below:

- **How my destination aligns with my values:**

_____

_____

_____

By connecting your goals to your values, you ensure that the destination resonates with what truly matters to you, making the journey more fulfilling and meaningful.

The Destination - Value

The meaning of a destination lies in what it represents to us—how it aligns with our self-view and what it signifies about our growth. Goals are more than just checkpoints; they're reflections of what we hold dear and how we envision ourselves. But what happens when we reach the goal? Does the outcome define us, or is the fulfillment found in the process that got us there?

Consider this: You set a goal to lose weight. Once achieved, do you maintain the lifestyle that helped you succeed, or do you revert to old habits? Was the journey valuable enough to inspire lasting change? Or imagine working toward a promotion only to find the new role doesn't bring the satisfaction you expected. The true meaning of a goal isn't just about reaching it—it's about the transformation along the way.…

When we embrace the journey itself, it changes how we view the destination. Reaching the goal becomes a meaningful milestone rather than the sole measure of success. It brings a sense of purpose, helping us move forward to the next level—whether that's setting a new goal or continuing to grow in another area.

Marathoner's Revelation

Imagine Sarah, an aspiring marathon runner. For months, she trained tirelessly, waking up before dawn, braving the cold, and running countless miles. Her sights were set on crossing the finish line of her first marathon. It was the ultimate goal she believed would define her as a "real runner" and bring her the validation she craved.

On race day, Sarah lined up with thousands of other runners, nerves buzzing with anticipation. The first few miles flew by, her energy fueled by the cheering crowds. But around mile 18, exhaustion hit. Her legs felt like lead, and doubt crept into her mind. She thought, *What if I can't finish? What if I fail?*

Then something unexpected happened. She looked up and saw a fellow runner struggling but smiling, encouraging others as they passed. It struck Sarah that this race wasn't just about the finish line—it was about the effort, the camaraderie, and the strength she discovered in herself along the way.

With a new mindset, Sarah slowed her pace, adjusted her breathing, and started taking in her surroundings. She high-fived kids holding signs, thanked volunteers handing out water, and cheered on runners who needed encouragement. When she crossed the finish line, it wasn't the medal that brought tears to her eyes; it was the journey.

Later, reflecting on the race, Sarah realized the goal wasn't just completing 26.2 miles—it was the transformation she experienced during the process. The training taught her discipline, resilience, and the importance of finding joy even in challenging moments. The race day struggles showed her the power of community and gratitude.

The marathon was a milestone, but the real success was embracing the journey. It shifted her focus from proving her worth to herself and others to celebrating her growth and the experiences that brought her there.

Reframing Success

A key question to ask yourself is: What is beyond the goal? Does achieving it make you something more, or do you recognize that your value has always been inherent, independent of the outcome? Your worth is not something to be earned or proven—it exists regardless of success or failure. This shift in perspective allows us to find fulfillment in the process and release the need to prove our worth.

True success isn't about simply reaching a destination; it's about living with purpose, meaning, and passion. When we tie our self-worth to outcomes, we risk falling into what I call the "victory response"—that nagging voice that downplays every success:

"Yes, but it could have been better."
"Yes, but I had help."
"Yes, but it's not enough."

This mindset creates a cycle of dissatisfaction, where even our victories feel hollow. To break free, we must recognize that our worth isn't tied to what we achieve. It's rooted in who we are and the purpose we bring to our journey.

The goal matters, but how we pursue it—the intention, growth, and fulfillment we experience along the way—is what truly changes our lives.

Your Inherent Value

We are not defined by outcomes. Think of Thomas Edison, who failed over 10,000 times before perfecting the lightbulb, or Christopher Columbus, whose miscalculations led to an unintended discovery. These examples remind us that success isn't about perfection—it's about perseverance, learning, and contribution.

Our struggles and failures are not signs of inadequacy but stepping stones to growth and purpose.

The beauty of goals is that we define them. We control how we experience the journey and how we interpret the destination.

It is my prayer that everyone reading this book already knows this, but it's worth taking a moment to mention: Not only is the journey inherently valuable, but YOU are inherently valuable. You are unique and have something to contribute.

This doesn't mean perfection is required. Part of embracing your worth is humbly accepting your flaws—acknowledging them without using them as weapons against yourself. Growth comes not from tearing yourself down, but from learning, adjusting, and moving forward with grace. Your flaws do not diminish your worth; they simply make you human.

Take a moment and close your eyes. **Own it. Breathe it. Take it in.**

Your value is not dependent on how others see you. Your value is not dependent on what your goal is, or even if you reach it.

What *does* change is your own experience of your daily existence. What changes is your sense of fulfillment and purpose.

What I pray for you is a **big and dynamic existence defined by YOU.**

The Destination – Where

Deciding where you want to go might seem straightforward at first. But as you reflect, it often becomes more nuanced than it initially appears. If you're an experienced journey planner with a clear vision and established goals, you might be what we'll call a **"Goal Manager."** This part of the journey may feel more natural for you—you likely see each successive goal as a step along a well-lit path. Even so, you may still benefit from the visualization exercises provided later in this chapter to refine and deepen your focus.

On the other hand, if you find it challenging to set a goal or bring it to completion, you may resonate more with the traits of a **Goal Keeper** or a **Goal Seeker.** This doesn't mean you're behind—it simply means your strengths and growth opportunities lie elsewhere. For you, this chapter may require some extra time and reflection, but it will ultimately help you clarify your direction and bring your goals to life.

The Goal Keeper

If you identify as a Goal Keeper, you're likely overflowing with ideas and interests. Your creativity and ability to envision possibilities are gifts, but they can also make it difficult to choose a single path forward. You might feel paralyzed by the fear of losing some of those brilliant ideas if you don't act on all of them. This abundance of possibilities can sometimes prevent any of them from taking complete shape.

Here's the good news: You don't have to give up any of your ideas. All things are possible, even the ones that feel improbable right now. Start by gathering your thoughts. Write them down in your *Embrace the Journey Planner*, a notebook, or even on a vision board. Keep the list alive by adding new ideas as they come. This exercise frees you to focus on one goal at a time without fear of losing the others.

Visualization Exercise for Goal Keepers

This exercise works well with a trusted friend, accountability partner, or mentor who can observe your body language and reactions. If you're self-directing, stay mindful of your own physical and emotional responses.

1. Sit comfortably, close your eyes, and let your mind drift freely.

2. Visualize each of your ideas one at a time.

3. Ask yourself: Does this align with my values?

4. If the answer is yes, explore the goal further: What would it look like to achieve this? What challenges might arise, and how do they make you feel?

5. As you visualize, pay attention to your physical responses—do you feel energized, calm, or tense? Does one idea ignite more excitement or passion than the others?

Once you've completed this process, narrow your focus to one or two goals. Write them down as your immediate priorities. The remaining ideas can be safely "bracketed" for later. List them on your "Big Ideas" page in your *Embrace the Journey Planner*. This approach allows you to honor all your aspirations while making meaningful progress on the ones that matter most right now.

Write it out here:

The Goal Seeker

If you're a Goal Seeker, you may find yourself unsure of what you truly want or how to define your purpose. It might feel like there's a tether tied to your ankle, holding you back from reaching your dreams. You're not alone in this. Life's responsibilities and obligations often drown out the voice of our inner selves, making it harder to uncover our desires.

This process of discovery might take time, but it's a journey worth taking. To begin, let's explore who you were before the noise of daily life overshadowed your inner voice.

Visualization Exercise for Goal Seekers

1. Sit comfortably and close your eyes.

2. Let your mind travel back to your earliest memories. What brought you joy or excitement as a child?

3. Were you drawn to animals, art, or science? Did you love creating, exploring, or solving problems?

4. Focus on those moments and let them guide you toward what still resonates today.

For example, as a child, I loved people watching. I would beg my grandfather to take me to the airport just so I could observe the travelers and imagine their stories. That fascination grew into an interest in psychology as I got older.

Moving Forward

If your reflections still feel incomplete, consider taking a personality or skills assessment, such as DISC or Myers-Briggs. These tools can offer valuable insights and might even spark ideas for goals you hadn't considered.

Start with small, manageable steps. For instance, if you struggle with self-care, begin by scheduling time for yourself each week. Even if you don't yet know your destination, taking intentional steps forward will help the road ahead unfold.

Remember, you don't have to embark on this journey alone. Joining a success group or partnering with a trusted accountability buddy can provide encouragement and inspiration. Sometimes, the creativity and energy of others can help you find clarity in your own path.

Whether you're managing multiple goals or seeking your first step forward, this chapter is your opportunity to focus, reflect, and move closer to a life defined by your purpose and passions.

Embrace the Journey: Finding Joy in the Process

It's time to embrace the journey! Whether your goal is starting a business, learning an instrument, prioritizing health, or simply taking better care of yourself, the process is where the true magic happens.

Have you ever noticed that the most inspiring stories often come from those who have faced adversity or overcome great obstacles? Their power comes from their ability to embrace the journey—the ups, downs, and everything in between. They took what served them, let go of what didn't, and moved forward with purpose.

Part of embracing the journey is embracing yourself—your identity, values, and purpose. It's about breaking free from the opinions and boxes others may try to place you in. Remember, there is no box unless you create one. No one but you, defines who you are. God created you to live fully, as your best and truest self.

So, go all in. Do you, in the biggest way possible. Open your mind and heart to the vision God has placed on your heart, and let it guide you.

Yes, there will be trade-offs along the way. A mom who leaves her career to homeschool might feel conflicted about finances. A business executive might wrestle with sacrificing family time to advance their career. Here's the truth: *Internal conflict obscures joy and purpose.* Everything has a cost—a "mixed bag," so to speak. Once you've made your decision, let go of the conflict and fully embrace the road you've chosen.

Your journey is uniquely yours. And this book will guide you through the mental and practical preparation to embrace the process and reach your destination.

Goal Stoppers: Overcoming the Obstacles to Progress

Every journey has its challenges, and the path to achieving your goals is no different. While your goals are worth striving for, the road to them isn't always smooth. Sometimes, we encounter obstacles—big and small—that can slow us down, distract us, or even make us question whether we should keep going.

These "goal stoppers" aren't signs that you've failed; they're part of the process. The key is recognizing them for what they are: opportunities to learn, adapt, and grow stronger.

In this section, we'll explore some of the most common barriers people face on their journey to success, from a hazy sense of purpose to the fear of failure or the temptation of distractions. Along the way, you'll learn how to identify these challenges, confront them with clarity, and stay on track toward your goals.

Road Hazards: Enthusiasm vs. Passion

Some obstacles aren't obvious at first—they look like opportunities. Imagine driving down a road and spotting a side path that seems to lead in the right direction. You think, *Why not?* Let's explore a little. It feels adventurous and exciting. But before you know it, you're lost, miles off course, and frustrated at the detour.

This is how enthusiasm can masquerade as passion. It's easy to get caught up in the energy of a trend, group, or program that promises success. Society often pressures us to follow a set path or adopt others' definitions of achievement. You might hear things like, *"If you don't join ____, you're not serious about your goals."*

While these groups or trends may hold value for some, they might not align with your core purpose. Enthusiasm is surface-level—it excites us in the moment. Passion, on the other hand, is deeply tied to our essence and what brings us lasting fulfillment.

For example, here's how I distinguish the two in my own life:

- Enthusiasm: The beach, self-help programs, real estate, organizing, teaching.

- Passion: Animals, nutritional and herbal medicine, family, coaching, freedom, and God.

Both are valuable, but my passions drive my long-term goals.

To stay true to your journey, ask yourself: *Am I pursuing a goal that aligns with my passions, or am I chasing temporary enthusiasm?* Focus on the goals that resonate with your deepest values, and remember—it's okay to bracket other interests for later.

Common Goal Stoppers

Here are some of the most frequent challenges people face on their journey to success, along with tips to overcome them.

1. Hazy or Undefined Purpose ("Why")

Your purpose is your compass. Without a clear "why," it's easy to lose motivation when challenges arise. A superficial purpose—like achieving a goal because it seems like the "right" thing to do, or because it was "expected" of you—won't sustain you through the hard times.

Ask yourself: *What truly drives me?* Your "why" should be personal, meaningful, and aligned with your values. Maybe you want to inspire your children, solve a problem you're passionate about, or honor the people who believed in you.

Motivational Insight:
A strong "why" doesn't just keep you moving—it becomes the heartbeat of your journey. When the path feels unclear or overwhelming, your purpose pulls you forward like a lifeline in the fog. Even if your "why" starts small, let it take root. The clarity will grow as you walk. You don't need to have it all figured out—you just need to care enough to begin looking.

Action Step:
Reflect on your story. What brings you joy? What experiences have shaped your passions? If your "why" isn't clear, make finding it your first goal. Remember: A strong "why" doesn't just guide you; it adds value to the journey itself.

2. Procrastination: Waiting for the Perfect Time

Procrastination is often rooted in fear—fear of failure, fear of success, or fear of the unknown. We tell ourselves, *I'll start when I have more time, money, or resources.* But waiting for the perfect time is a trap. There is no perfect time—there's only now.

Motivational Insight:
You're not lazy—you're likely just scared. But here's the secret: movement shrinks fear. Action, even messy or imperfect, proves to your brain that you're capable. You don't need to leap a mountain—just take the next right step. Courage builds in motion, not stillness. Starting now—even in a small way—is the most powerful choice you can make.

Action Step:
Face procrastination head-on. If time or money feels like a barrier, ask yourself: *What can I do with what I have right now?* Can't afford a program? Borrow a book from the library or watch a free tutorial online. The smallest steps forward build momentum, and momentum builds success.

3. Lack of a Plan

Think of a vacation. Would you set out without knowing your destination or packing the essentials? Probably not. Goals are no different. A clear plan outlines your steps, reduces stress, and increases your chances of success. Without one, you risk wandering aimlessly or losing motivation.

Motivational Insight:
Dreams don't need perfect blueprints to become real—they just need commitment. A plan is not a prison; it's a pathway. It creates direction without trapping your creativity. When you give your dream a map, even a rough one, you begin to shift from wishful thinking to forward momentum. You don't need the whole staircase—just the first few steps.

Action Step:
Break your goal into smaller, actionable steps. Use the *Embrace the Journey Planner* to map out milestones and timelines. A good plan doesn't have to be perfect—it just has to guide you forward.

4. Expecting Instant Gratification

In a world of quick rewards, it's easy to grow impatient when success takes time. But lasting achievements often require persistence. Without immediate results, you might dismiss your goal as "sour grapes" and give up.

Motivational Insight:
True success is about the process, not just the prize. Surround yourself with supportive people who remind you of your progress. Celebrate small wins—they're proof you're moving in the right direction.

Action Step:
Give yourself permission to celebrate the small wins and the completed mini-steps in the process. Let the smallest positive help drive you forward to bigger steps and greater progress. Let yourself feel the accomplishment of each stage of the journey.

5. Not Anticipating Storms and "Ticks"

Storms and setbacks are inevitable. They might feel like hitting brick walls that stop you in your tracks. But challenges are not roadblocks—they're opportunities to grow stronger and more resourceful.

Motivational Insight:
When the rain falls, put on your jacket and grab your umbrella. Keep going. Each storm you weather brings you closer to your goal.

Action Step:
List potential challenges you might face and brainstorm potential solutions. Prepare your "rain gear" now so you're ready when the storm comes. Think "how", not "if" or "maybe". Always look for a way around, over or under any problem.

6. Bad Habits and Viewing Mistakes as Failures

Old habits and negative self-talk can sabotage your progress. Telling yourself, *I can't because I'm too ___ (old, slow, busy, etc.)* reinforces false beliefs. Mistakes, too, can feel like failures—but they're not. Mistakes are proof you're trying.

Motivational Insight:
Change begins with your mindset. Instead start with "I choose". When we recognize we choose our responses, where we put our time, what we make a priority, it changes the dynamic completely. Replace "I can't" with "I can," and focus on the possibilities. As Anne of Green Gables reminds us, "Tomorrow is a new day with no mistakes in it… yet."

Action Step:
Identify one habit or belief holding you back and replace it with a positive action or affirmation. Give yourself grace, and remember: The journey is not about perfection; it's about progress.

7. Lack of Scheduling

We make time for what matters to us. When you commit your time to your goals, you signal their importance to yourself and those around you. If scheduling feels hard, it might indicate a deeper hesitation about your goal or your "why."

Motivational Insight:
Scheduling doesn't have to be exact hours. Scheduling or blocking time can look like setting aside "mornings" for more complex tasks when you are fresh. Determining you'll work 3 days a week at least a couple hours each day on something, but based upon your "best" time of day. Setting goals within those time frames help move you forward and helps you keep motivated.

Action Step:
Schedule dedicated time for your goal in your planner. Treat it as non-negotiable, just like a doctor's appointment. Taking control of your time is an act of self-respect and empowerment.

8. Fear

Fear is sneaky and sly. It often hides itself as doubt, blame, excuses, or even procrastination. Its roots can run deep—fear of failure, fear of success, fear of being seen. It can paralyze you if left unchecked. But here's the truth: Fear loses its power when you face it head-on.

Motivational Insight:
Courage doesn't mean being fearless—it means acting despite fear. Search to see past it. Be open. Confront and name the fear. You've overcome challenges before and you can do it again. Sometimes being able to see past a fear allows you to plan ahead and avoid the very issue completely!

Action Step:
Write down your fears and where they might be coming from. Acknowledge them, then ask yourself: *What's the worst that could happen?* Often, you'll realize the fear is bigger in your mind than in reality. Ask yourself if there are steps you can take that would side-step the issue. If it's internal, look for the source and realize fear is a **liar**, every, single, time. This is where an accountability partner can assist as well.

9. Inflexibility

Rigidity is the enemy of progress. When we cling to a perfect plan, any deviation can feel like failure. But flexibility allows us to adapt and find new solutions when things don't go as expected.

Motivational Insight:
Think of your goal as a destination and your plan as a route. If one road is blocked, take a detour. The journey may look different, but you'll still get where you're going.

Action Step:
Identify areas where you can be more flexible. Practice reframing challenges as opportunities to think creatively.

10. Losing Focus

Focus determines your direction. When your thoughts stray to negativity or distractions, it's like a car drifting off the road. Remember: *We go where we focus.*

Motivational Insight:
Staying focused isn't about perfection—it's about gently choosing your path again and again. Every time you redirect your attention toward your goal, you're building strength, resilience, and momentum. Even a small shift in focus can change the course of your entire journey. Keep choosing forward.

Action Step:
Visualize your goal daily. Keep reminders—like sticky notes or vision boards—where you can see them. When distractions arise, gently bring your focus back to your desired destination.

11. Not Creating Your Environment

Your environment plays a crucial role in your success. Without the right tools, atmosphere, or support, even the best intentions can falter. The spaces we spend time in either feed our growth or drain our energy. From the people we allow around us to the clutter (or calm) on our desks, every detail influences our mindset and momentum. A chaotic or uninspiring environment can silently sabotage your efforts, while a purposeful, uplifting space can anchor your focus and breathe life into your goals.

Motivational Insight:
You don't have to wait for the perfect conditions—create them. Curating your environment is an act of commitment to your future self. When you build a space that reflects where you're going, not where you've been, you give your goals a home to grow in.

Action Step:
Set up a space that supports your goal. Whether it's a study area, a workout corner, or a quiet zone for reflection: create an environment that inspires and motivates you.

12. No Accountability Partner

Success is easier with support. An accountability partner provides encouragement, perspective, and motivation to keep you on track. We weren't meant to do everything alone. Having someone walk alongside you—someone who believes in your vision and won't let you quit when things get tough—can be the difference between staying stuck and moving forward.

Motivational Insight:
Accountability isn't just about checking in; it's about being seen, supported, and reminded that your goals matter. When someone else holds space for your success, it becomes easier to show up for yourself, too.

Action Step:
Share your goal with someone you trust and ask them to check in with you regularly. Or join a group where you can give and receive support.

13. Forgetting to Celebrate Victories

Every step forward is worth celebrating. Recognizing your progress boosts your confidence and keeps you motivated for the journey ahead. Success creates more success!

Motivational Insight: Celebration is fuel for the soul. When you take time to acknowledge even the smallest wins, you reinforce your progress and remind yourself that you *are* moving forward. It shifts your mindset from chasing an outcome to appreciating the process. Joy grows when we notice it. So clap for yourself, cheer yourself on, and let those little victories light the way to the big ones.

Action Step:
Plan small rewards for each milestone you achieve. Savor the moments—they're part of the joy of the journey.

Embracing the Journey

Each of these challenges is part of the process. They don't define you—they refine you. With awareness, persistence, and the right tools, you can overcome any goal stopper in your path. Remember: *The power is ours. We choose.*

PLANNING

Planning is the bridge between where you are and where you want to go. It's the phase where you take your dreams and transform them into actionable steps. Whether your goals are personal, professional, or somewhere in between, this section equips you with the tools to navigate your path with clarity and confidence.

We'll start by gaining a clear understanding of your current situation—*your lay of the land*. From there, we'll explore how to chart your course, anticipate obstacles, and prepare for the unexpected. You'll learn how to budget resources, choose your "travel partners," and even "pack" the essentials for your journey.

Planning doesn't have to feel overwhelming. Think of it as your adventure blueprint, where every detail adds richness to the experience. Let's dive in and start building the foundation for your success.

Lay of the Land

The phrase *lay of the land* means gaining knowledge or insight about your current position and the journey ahead. This is where you assess the situation as it stands right now, compare it to your intended destination, and identify the steps needed to bridge the gap.

Imagine your goal is earning a master's degree. You'd begin by evaluating your current education level, understanding the prerequisites for your desired program, and determining which schools align with your focus, passion, schedule, and finances. Do you need to take prerequisite classes, secure funding, or research which programs meet your long-term goals? This process ensures that you're prepared to start your journey and stay on course.

By gaining a comprehensive view of your starting point, you'll also be able to anticipate potential challenges. For instance, if a subject doesn't come naturally to you, you may plan extra study time or seek additional support. Seeing the "lay of the land" helps you avoid false expectations and unnecessary missteps. But then not every journey is expected or visible…

What if you feel like you have no idea what to expect ahead? Does that mean you can't get started? Of course not! Let's go! One foot in front of the other, just focus on the next step, then the next, and so on. At each stage the next step will present itself. Did Frodo or Bilbo know what they were headed into? The terrain they would cover? They just knew the path might be difficult. So whatever comes your way, pretend you are Emmitt Smith of the Cowboys and keep those feet moving no matter what!

Road Conditions Ahead

Just like planning a road trip, understanding the "road conditions" ahead can prevent detours and delays. Knowing you might need rain, snow or all terrain tires can ease the way. Let's consider a business example: Imagine you're launching a new product. Your "lay of the land" would include evaluating your target market, analyzing competitors, and identifying potential supply chain issues. What obstacles might you face? Perhaps there's a lack of market awareness, logistical hiccups, or unforeseen costs. By preparing ahead, you can plan marketing strategies, secure alternative suppliers, and budget for contingencies.

Or, in real estate, think of an agent aiming to build their client base. The agent might start by assessing their current network and identifying gaps. They'd research market trends, demographics, and preferred communication methods for prospective clients. For instance, if a neighborhood is trending with first-time homebuyers, the agent might tailor their approach with educational resources or workshops. Preparing in this way provides an opportunity to adapt as needed and increases the likelihood of reaching their goals.

Imagine a busy entrepreneur aiming to improve their health and fitness. Their "lay of the land" might include evaluating their current physical activity level, daily schedule, and dietary habits.

- What's working? Perhaps they already enjoy a morning walk.

- What's not working? Maybe long work hours leave them relying on fast food.

With this knowledge, they can map out a plan: scheduling gym visits, prepping healthy meals on Sundays, or using a fitness tracker to monitor progress. Challenges (road conditions) like fatigue or time constraints are anticipated and countered with strategies like shorter, high-intensity workouts or hiring a meal delivery service.

By integrating these solutions into their routine they not only avoid pitfalls, but also enhance their enjoyment of the process.

The Journey is an Evolving Landscape

The "lay of the land" is not a one-time exercise—it's a continual process. Just like driving, you'll need to keep an eye on the road ahead while staying aware of your surroundings. Oncoming traffic, road signs, and potential hazards require your attention, just as life's ever-changing circumstances will require adjustments to your plan.

As a real estate agent, rules change, forms change, and what clients are looking for can change. Buyers wanted open floor plans for many years, but now trends are shifting to accommodate multi-generational households and working at home. Clients used to walk-in to "brick and mortar" locations and now they find their homes and their agents online, or by referral. This industry tends to be an ever-evolving landscape that requires continual education and adjustments.

Consider being a parent navigating your children's education. School choice bills are being passed, some parents are moving to home schooling, and instead of nuclear attack drills – kids are now taught drills for armed intruders. The debates and rules are constantly changing as kids change and as they grow. I have friends who have varied their children's education over the years sometimes going between state schools and homeschooling. Why? Because their children experienced different needs at different ages, because the family's situation altered, or location changed.

Have you ever noticed while driving through states across our country that many have extremely different landscapes in different areas within the state? Each brings its own beauty and its own challenges.

Consider this: Adaption to change is a powerful skill. As a new driver, juggling multiple inputs might feel overwhelming. With practice, however, it becomes second nature. Similarly, as you develop the habit of assessing and adapting to your current situation, you'll find it easier to navigate your journey with confidence.

Know Thyself

Part of getting the lay of the land is understanding what *you* bring to the table. Reflect on your strengths, tendencies, and potential challenges. For example, if you thrive in structured environments, you might schedule activities meticulously. If spontaneity energizes you, you might plan for flexibility.

As human beings one of the greatest things we can do for ourselves, as well as those around us, is to take time to get to know ourselves. What brings you satisfaction, what helps you feel accomplished, what drives you crazy, what brings you peace? What triggers you and upsets your emotions?

Being authentically open here, I'll share a bit of my own journey: I have what I call a "justice meter". If I see an injustice, especially to someone I care about, it's a trigger. It can drive me to distraction until I deal with it. I know I work better on more difficult tasks when I'm fresh during the morning, and I get more accomplished on creative energy tasks in the evening. I can actually see a difference in my writing tone between morning and evening projects! I also know I tend to be full of ideas, so I've learned how to bracket them as they come up so I can continue working on today's project. Lastly, I know my powerhouse move is to have a support staff that is fantastic at filling my weak spots and anticipating my needs. It allows me to keep going full steam ahead with less distraction or side trips.

This honest self-assessment is a powerful tool. When you know your natural responses and work style, you can anticipate and address potential pitfalls. Look at your "untwisted truth." This isn't about judgment. It's about empowerment. Seeing yourself clearly (even your weaknesses—sometimes *especially* those) helps you avoid obstacles and maximize opportunities.

Make It Fun

Who wants to dredge through their day? How many of us face the workday without any anticipation or excitement? It's a chore to get through any way we can. There tends to be two types of approaches. One way sees every chore as something to barely manage to get through. Everything difficult is to be avoided or endured. The other way sees every challenge as something to overcome with excitement. This way makes every chore fun in whatever way they can. Whether it becomes a contest with oneself, singing while we work or trying to beat the clock… Bring fun into it.

Pretend you're researching a town you'll pass through on a road trip. What attractions or activities can you include to make the journey more enjoyable? Apply this same sense of curiosity and adventure to your goals. Whether it's finding tools to streamline your progress or incorporating hobbies that bring joy, embrace the process.

Questions to Consider:

- What do I need to research?

- What activities or environment will enhance my journey?

- What steps will directly support my goal?

The more intentional and prepared you are, the richer your experience will be. Your journey is yours to create—so why not make it as fulfilling and exciting as possible?

Trip Plan

Some road trips leave you meandering between destinations with no real purpose in mind. It can be enjoyable but there is generally no specific outcome planned. Usually, on a road trip you are at least planning the next leg of your journey by looking at the maps and deciding where you want to go next. Some people plan every aspect so that they maximize the journey and the accomplishments/destinations on the way.

You may not know every step and can't anticipate everything that will happen along the way, but you can create an outline based on where you are starting and where you'd like to end up. Planning can help you maintain your overall direction and help you discern if you are still on the right path even when the unexpected happens. It can help you recenter when you are out of sync.

Embarking on the journey toward your goals requires planning and a flexible mindset. As you chart your course, it's essential to recognize that change is an inherent part of the process. Many authors have delved into the complexities of change, offering insights that can guide us through transitions.

For instance, in "Managing Transitions: Making the Most of Change," William Bridges emphasizes the psychological adjustments individuals undergo during change and provides strategies to navigate these transitions effectively.

Similarly, "Switch: How to Change Things When Change Is Hard" by Chip Heath and Dan Heath explores how to effect transformative change by understanding the balance between rational and emotional forces.

Change can indeed challenge our self-perception. When we alter aspects of our lives, especially in response to challenges or setbacks, it can unsettle our established identity. This disruption may lead to self-doubt or resistance, as we grapple with reconciling our past self with new realities.

Brené Brown, in "The Gifts of Imperfection," discusses how embracing vulnerability and letting go of the need for perfection can lead to a more authentic self. She highlights that change often requires us to confront our imperfections, which can be uncomfortable but ultimately liberating.

Understanding that change can threaten our self-view is crucial. It allows us to approach transitions with compassion and self-awareness, acknowledging the discomfort while remaining committed to growth. By reframing change as an opportunity to evolve rather than a threat to our identity, we can navigate the journey with resilience and openness.

As you prepare for potential challenges—those anchor points that may hinder your progress—remember that adaptability and self-awareness are your allies. Embrace the journey, knowing that each step, whether smooth or rocky, contributes to your personal and professional development.

Beware of "Anchor Points"

Every journey has its challenges—those things that weigh us down, slow our progress, or keep us tethered in one place when we should be moving forward. Let's call these challenges **"anchor points"**. Like a ship anchored in a harbor, these points can hold us back, keeping us from exploring the vast open waters ahead.

Anchor points come in many forms. Some are external, like difficult circumstances or unexpected setbacks. Others are internal, stemming from our fears, habits, or self-doubt. Just like an anchor can keep a ship steady in rough waters, these challenges can have both positive and negative effects—depending on how we address them.

When we ignore them, these anchor points become dead weight dragging us down and depleting our energy. But when we identify them and deal with them directly, they can become a source of strength and growth, helping us navigate through life's storms.

Anchors Within: Confronting Internal Challenges

Sometimes the heaviest anchor points are the ones inside us. These could be habits we've clung to for years, fears we haven't faced, or beliefs that don't serve us anymore. Change threatens our self-view because it forces us to question the stories we tell ourselves about who we are.

For instance, someone might believe their worth depends on always getting everything right. If they don't, they feel it makes them worthy of rejection—and that's where perfectionism is born. A change—like taking on a new role or pursuing a goal outside their comfort zone—can challenge their self-view. What happens when things aren't perfect? Does it mean they've failed? Does it mean they're not enough?

What about the "I can't" self-messages, or the "that's just the way I am", as if it's a final sentence from which you can never grow or change. It may bring us some sense of comfort to excuse ourselves, but it also perpetuates failure and a negative self-view. Our subconscious knows the truth and it creates internal conflict.

In his book *Mindset: The New Psychology of Success*, Dr. Carol Dweck explores how adopting a growth mindset—believing that abilities and intelligence can be developed—can transform our response to challenges. She explains that when we see change as an opportunity for growth, rather than a threat, we're better equipped to navigate the discomfort and uncertainty it brings.

The truth is, confronting internal anchor points takes real courage. It means slowing down long enough to listen to the quiet parts of ourselves—the beliefs we've carried for years, sometimes without even realizing it. It requires self-reflection, honesty, and a willingness to look inward without judgment. That's no small thing. It's easy to stay busy or distracted, but growth demands that we face ourselves, even the parts we'd rather avoid. This kind of inner work is a powerful form of self-love: not the fluffy kind, but the kind that roots deep. It's acknowledging both our strengths and the places where we still have work to do—without shame, without harshness. It's holding space for our humanity while remembering, always, that our value isn't tied to perfection. Growth doesn't mean becoming flawless; it means becoming more whole.

External Anchors: Overcoming Practical Challenges

Not all anchor points are internal. Sometimes, the challenges we face are practical, like a lack of resources, time, or skills. When we know we have everything we need to accomplish our goals except_____ (money, time, staff, resources, materials, etc.), we can feel frustrated and like we are stuck in place. Not knowing how to get what we need feels even worse. This is the moment when we need to ask for help. We may turn to a mentor or accountability partner, we may ask other experts, ask Google or even Chat GPT, read a book, or look for a partner who perhaps has what we lack.

Let's consider an example from business: Imagine a real estate agent who is exceptional at closing deals but struggles with social media. They find themselves overwhelmed, stressed, and distracted from their core work—connecting with clients and selling homes. This anchor point is holding them back.

The solution? They assess their options: Do they invest time in learning social media themselves, or do they hire a professional to handle it? By outsourcing this task, they free up their energy for what they love and do best. Letting go of tasks that weigh us down isn't a sign of weakness—it's a strategic choice to focus on our strengths and move forward.

Sometimes, it's a matter of reallocating our resources from one location to another. Perhaps spending time on our goal instead of on the weekend game with friends. If there is something lacking, an important question to ask is, "How do I get what I need?"

None of us lives in a vacuum, and connection is a part of our daily lives. Connecting with a group, partner or mentor that can help you strategize to overcome external anchors is a priceless step indeed. The key is to recognize that needing help doesn't mean you're deficient; it means you're human.

Turning Anchors into Opportunities

Anchor points don't define us—they challenge us to grow. They provide opportunity. As a Star Trek geek, the term "opportunity" makes me think of the Ferengi, who always looked for opportunity in every situation. When we address anchors head-on, they become opportunities for self-discovery and transformation.

Authentic openness here… I tried to go into business with someone who I realized too late was not a good match. We did not have the same values. We thought we had the same vision, but it turned out our level of dedication and the "how" we were going to get there were continents apart, and there was no bringing us together. As a result, I lost time, money, confidence and had a miserable couple of years. Yet, that time turned into some of the greatest personal growth I've ever experienced. I learned things I never dreamed I needed to know, and that now serves me in every business and goal I'm working on today. Overcoming that challenge and negative relationship was priceless. Painful, yes. Horrific, yes. But priceless!

There are many ways we can turn challenges or even defeat into opportunity. Consider someone who struggles with public speaking. They might view it as an anchor point that limits their career potential. By taking small, consistent steps—like joining a supportive group such as Toastmasters—they can transform that anchor into a skill. Over time, what once held them back becomes a source of confidence and accomplishment.

Taking consistent small steps can lead us to greater and greater growth and opportunities. The same applies to overcoming perfectionism, procrastination, and self-doubt. Each small step forward weakens the hold of the anchor, allowing you to set sail toward your goals.

Practical Steps to Deal with Anchor Points

1. **Identify the Anchor**
   What's holding you back? Is it a skill you lack, a fear you haven't addressed, or a habit that's no longer serving you? Write it down. Naming the anchor is the first step to removing it.

2. **Decide How to Address It**
   Do you need to invest time in learning a new skill, or is this something you can delegate? For example, if you struggle with organization, could a planner or a coach help you create systems that work for you?

3. **Ask for Help**
   If the anchor feels too heavy to lift on your own, reach out. A mentor, coach, or friend can provide the perspective and support you need. Remember, no one succeeds alone.

4. **Celebrate Small Wins**
   Each time you loosen the grip of an anchor point, celebrate it. Progress is progress, no matter how small.

Letting Go Without Regret

When we let go of what no longer serves us—whether it's a task, a habit, or an outdated belief—we create space for growth. There's value in the struggle, but there's also value in releasing it when the time comes. It can be any type of anchor that we let go of.

Perhaps at one point stubbornness was a quality that saved you from being bullied or intimidated by others. Now, as you've grown, you can stand up for yourself while still staying open to new thoughts and ideas that might serve you. The purpose of being stubborn served you at the time, but in and of itself it is not the answer.

Maybe it's the opposite... Being timid and quiet saved you suffering at some point in your life. Avoiding conflict was akin to survival. But today, it may keep you from feeling a sense of security and freedom. It may keep you from what is due to you such as respect, or even income.

Sometimes, letting go means releasing the vision of how we thought it would look – whether that's the journey or the destination. Maybe, we need to let go of a task that is better suited to outsourcing to someone with greater skill in that area.

Letting go of our ego is one of the hardest, yet most rewarding steps to personal growth and reaching our goals. Letting go of ego doesn't mean you stop caring or lose your voice—it just means you stop needing to be right all the time, stop trying to control what others think, and stop chasing validation. Ego wants to protect our image, but it usually ends up getting in the way of the real work—growth, healing, and connection. When we let it go, even a little, things feel lighter. More honest. More grounded. It's not about shrinking back; it's about showing up without the mask.

Letting go of ego, and embracing the process frees you from the burden of insecurity, perfectionism, or the need to prove yourself.

As you navigate your journey, remember this: *Your value is inherent. You are enough.*

Navigating the Rough Waters

Dealing with anchor points is about removing what holds us back. But what happens when the journey itself gets rough—when we're knocked off course by unexpected storms? That's where resilience and adaptability come in.

Just like ships encounter storms on their journey, we too face storms that test our strength—and far too often, we find ourselves clinging to the very anchors that are keeping us from moving forward. There are many storms that come up in life, but here are a few examples as you reflect on your own.

- **The Storm of Sudden Loss**
  The unexpected death of a loved one or the loss of a job can feel like being caught in a hurricane with no warning. Grief and uncertainty can act as anchors, making it hard to move forward—but they can also open us up to deep reflection, newfound priorities, and a greater sense of purpose if we allow ourselves to heal.

  In my youth, I lost my job unexpectedly. I'd really struggled with the job due to the manager's treatment of staff, limited leadership and tendency to go out of her way to humiliate staff she saw as "below" her station. I had focused on rising above her behavior and it drove me to do my best to be above reproach. I prayed my way though that job and then to lose it seemed a slap in the face. During the time (and it did take some time to get another position) I was jobless, I remember the usual depression, struggle, questions as to why, etc. But truth was, it drove me to find something more fulfilling. I ended up with a new job, better pay, better working environment and an employer that truly valued my contributions. In fact, he invested back into me with education, self-growth classes and training that exceeded the scope of the position I was in.

It doesn't minimize the struggle in the moment at all. We can both struggle with a loss, and we can use it to drive us forward at the same time. The loss of a loved one might drive us to serve a certain group in our community such as the elderly, or might drive us to start a charity, or it might bring us into closer relationship with other family members. It seems impossible to feel both pain, and fulfillment or purpose at the same time, but it is truly possible. Purpose and/or fulfillment helps us move past the tragedy.

- **The Storm of Burnout**
  Working tirelessly, always saying "yes," and trying to be everything to everyone can eventually spiral into exhaustion. You hit a wall. You can't move forward without reevaluating your boundaries, your identity, and where your value truly lies. Burnout may seem like a force trying to sink you—but it might just be the wake-up call that pushes you to re-anchor in self-care and intentional living.

Many years ago as I was a full-time college student, working full-time, married, and volunteering at my church. I existed on burnout. I had scheduled a trip to see my grandmother and family members, but by the time I reached them I was so exhausted that looking back on it now, I realize I was close to collapse. Wonderfully, my family understood and gave me the support and space to take that time to rest and just enjoy their company, without any demands or expectations.

For some of us, this issue can be a circular pattern that repeats over the years. And truthfully, it has been for me. I do catch on to it quicker than I did in my youth, and I consciously work towards balance now; however, it continues to be something I must be aware of and work on. I've had times in my life when getting 4 hours of sleep was a good night and I can truly say I was of no real benefit to anyone that mattered during that time. In fact, my business suffered right along with me.

- **The Storm of Failure**
  You launch a business or take a bold leap—and it flops. You poured your heart, soul, and savings into something that didn't work. The anchor here might be shame or fear of trying again. But facing failure, sitting in the wreckage, and learning from it, builds a stronger vessel for the next journey. Resilience is often born in the wreckage of the first storm.

Failure of relationships is one that can truly anchor us in place. We live in it, dwell on it, regret it, or when we are still feeling self-righteous, we live in anger about it. There are many ways a relationship can go wrong. Usually, at least on some level, it takes two. Relationships can be difficult to navigate in the best of times. Effects of a failed relationship can spill over into other people we know, such as kids, family and common friends, or if it's work related, into our business success as well. The other party might choose to "bad-talk" you to others and yes, many times unfairly.

With our greatest failures come some of our greatest lessons. We reveal our true character and strength in how we respond to these moments. We don't have to broadcast or justify what happened—our response alone becomes part of our testimony. How we carry ourselves during and after failure speaks volumes. Whether we choose grace, humility, reflection, or quiet resolve, our reaction shapes how others perceive the situation and, more importantly, how we grow from it. It affects how we move forward, how we heal, and what we're able to build from the wreckage. For example, we may recognize warning signs sooner next time or be more willing to speak up early rather than stay silent and let problems grow.

Let's not forget, there is power in remembering—many of the world's greatest breakthroughs were born through failure. Edison didn't get the lightbulb right the first time. It took thousands of missteps to illuminate the world. And Columbus? He may not have discovered what he set out to find, but his "failure" still changed the course of history. A misstep doesn't erase the significance of what comes from it. Sometimes, it's the unexpected outcome that holds the greatest value.

- **The Storm of Identity Shift**
  Becoming a parent. Changing careers. Ending a long-term relationship. These are just some of the potential life changes that can shake the very foundation of who we thought we were. It's easy to cling to the past of an old identity, routine, or role; like an anchor. However, true growth comes when we release who we were to embrace who we're becoming.

  Many first-time business owners experience difficulty in adjusting to their new identity shift. They have gone from being the "employee" to being the "boss". Yet, rarely is a new business owner prepared to take on all the aspects of that role. It means management level activities, such as bookkeeping, being your own HR department and handling your own employees, marketing, labor, complaint department, the scheduler and so on… They are wearing all the hats, all at once, without much time to adjust.

The best outcomes occur when they recognize the shift and take steps to address the new roles, and the new skills they will need to develop in order to be truly successful. Action steps in overcoming the inherent resistance to role change could be taking an HR or marketing class to fill gaps in their skill set. If finances allow, proactive business owners may hire to their greatest weakness, thereby strengthening their position in the marketplace.

- **The Storm of Rejection**
Not getting that job. Being left out of a group. Having your voice dismissed or overlooked. Rejection stings deeply—and it can linger far longer than we expect. It often plants a subtle but strong anchor: the belief that you are not enough.

But here's the truth: rejection often redirects us toward something more aligned with who we really are, or with the goals we are striving to accomplish. Seen through a growth lens, rejection becomes redirection.

The very personal pain of relational storms can turn into permanent anchors as we seek self-protection. For some people this leads them inward, shutting out any interactions that reinforce what they already feel: rejected and therefore inferior. Not good enough. Many times, a tendency to avoid confrontation goes along with this type of storm. They may begin to interpret silence or disagreement as rejection, reinforcing the belief that they're inferior, invisible, or unworthy. They become conflict-avoidant, choosing silence over discomfort.

Others may choose the opposite route. Bravado can be worn as a shield. As the flip side of internal shrinking, bravado is overly outgoing, pushy, talking over others, and acting like they live in their own world, oblivious to the reactions of those around them. Rooted in rejection, it's armor, not freedom. In both extremes, the rejection becomes the invisible chains by which everything we do is filtered through that one anchor.

The breakthrough comes when we step beyond it.

It may take time and great effort depending on the depth of the original wounds. Self-talk, stretching our comfort zones, taking a leap of faith for that next dream job, re-examining what we bring to the table for work skills, looking with open eyes at those who rejected us, can be steps along the path of letting it go.

Once we do, we can thrive in freedom from being held back by the fear of the next rejection. We can view it without injury to our ego. Our self-esteem can stay intact. And we can stand up for ourselves, embracing who we are in the moment without ourselves becoming arrogant or dismissive of others. We become rooted, not in defensiveness or people-pleasing, but in self-respect.

What power there is in that kind of freedom!

- **The Storm of Comparison**
  Especially in a world driven by social media, it's easy to look around and feel like everyone else is sailing smooth waters while we're stuck. That's a sneaky anchor point— comparison drains joy, creativity, and momentum. But confronting it head-on can shift focus inward (in a good way), back to your own unique journey.

As someone who works in the real estate industry, I see comparison everywhere—it's woven into nearly every part of the business. Many get stuck in the storm of comparison—whether it's newer agents measuring themselves against high producers, or top producers dismissing or looking down on those with less volume. But the truth is, this industry holds space and opportunity for professionals at every level.

I've seen high-producing, seasoned agents who know less and serve their clients less effectively than newer agents just starting out. It's a clear reminder: you truly can't judge a book by its cover. Every professional brings their own strengths and weaknesses to the table, and each business reflects the unique gifts of the person building it.

The beauty is that the single mom can work and take care of her children. The entrepreneur that doesn't have family and wants to work long hours can do so. People who walk all different sides of our culture can uniquely and wonderfully serve the public in the largest investment they'll ever make. The greatness of this business is that anyone can build their business the way they want. It can look how they want it to look. It can be as big or small as their needs may be at the time. Each agent can shine in their own unique way. Wonderous!

Yet, to get stuck in comparison is to rob ourselves of the joy and benefits of working in this industry and with the public we serve. It can stifle the best of the journey.

Consider the mom who's struggled with the weight change after having children? Some women seem to just melt off the pounds and look like they did prior to ever being pregnant and seem to do so with ease. However, some struggle with that part of the journey (for various reasons).

Comparison can rob these beautiful women of their satisfaction and joy at the role they are so brilliantly designed to fulfill.

Taking the time to recognize that our single view of others is only a limited one-direction, short sighted look in their direction, can help us let go of the need to compare. The truth is we don't know what the "behind the scenes" looks like. And, we may not even want the life someone else has if we could see all of it.

What we bring to this life is uniquely amazing and wonderful, and comparison robs us of our best selves. Let it go and find joy in who you are without regard to what others around you are doing.

- **The Storm of Silence**
Sometimes the storm doesn't come from chaos—but it rises from the quiet. The in-between seasons. The waiting. These are the moments where growth often happens below the surface. When no progress seems visible, it's tempting to anchor in discouragement. But often, it's the silence before a breakthrough.

You're showing up every day, doing your best, but nothing is shifting. Projects feel repetitive, recognition is scarce, and opportunities seem to have dried up. It feels like a standstill—but what's really happening is that your consistency, problem-solving, and reliability are quietly building a reputation. Leadership starts to notice not through fireworks, but through faithfulness. Then one day, out of nowhere, you're offered the promotion or asked to lead something new. What felt like silence was actually your resume being written—in real time.

As a Christ Follower, there can be periods when God seems silent, and it feels like you're just waiting in the in-between. No big signs. No clear answers. These times tend to come when we are most in need and we are looking for answers. The uncertainty is at best uncomfortable, and at worst it's nerve wracking. But in that stillness, trust is deepened. Patience grows. Faith takes root in a new way.

Maybe you're doing all the right things—reading, journaling, praying, working—but don't see outward results. What you don't see is how your character is being refined in that hidden place. It's like a seed under the soil—quiet, but not dormant.

Doubt as an Internal Storm

One of the most common storms we face is doubt. Doubt whispers that we're not good enough, not capable, or destined to fail. It creates false comparisons and negative self-talk that can derail even the most determined journey. Left unchecked, doubt can manifest as indecisiveness, self-sabotage, or even overachievement as a way for us to compensate.

To overcome doubt, it's essential to identify its source and replace it with truth. Doubt often stems from false beliefs formed during earlier experiences. Here's a chart to illustrate:

False Belief	Source	Possible Truth
"I'm not worth attention"	Ignored by a parent	"The parent was preoccupied, not a reflection of my worth."
"I'm inept"	Teased in school	"I was learning and growing like everyone else."
"I'm clumsy"	Fell during a childhood race	"I lacked experience, but can improve with practice."

False Belief	Source	Possible Truth
"I can't lead"	Failed group project	"Leadership is a skill I can develop over time."
"I'll never succeed"	Past failed attempts	"Every failure teaches me what doesn't work."

Protecting the Ego vs. Embracing Growth

Our ego, or self-view, plays a significant role in how we respond to storms. Sometimes we hold onto false beliefs to protect our self-image. For example, if we view ourselves as "not good at math," we might avoid situations where we could learn and grow, perpetuating that false belief. What does that look like? Whether it's your household budget and saving for retirement, or managing your business finances, that self-view can sabotage your goals and growth in the area of finance.

Ego protection can take two forms:

1. **Avoidance**: We steer clear of challenges that might reinforce our fears.

2. **Justification**: We create narratives to explain away shortcomings, even when growth is possible.

Neither of these options will lead us to the best result. Both will lead to inferior results and frustration, and even self-lies to protect our ego.

When we know our value is inherent—not tied to performance, perfection, or others' opinions—we're better equipped to face the hard stuff. Challenges to our self-view still sting, but they don't define us. Instead of shutting down when something threatens our sense of identity, we can lean in with curiosity. We stop seeing mistakes as proof that we're not enough, and start seeing them as invitations to grow. That shift matters. When you believe you are already enough at your core, you can survive the ego's discomfort. You can walk through failure, critique, even embarrassment—and come out stronger. That's when real transformation happens. Not because your ego was protected, but because your identity was secure enough to be stretched.

True growth requires letting go of our ego-driven defenses. When we embrace our inherent value, we recognize that making mistakes or facing challenges doesn't diminish who we are—it strengthens us. We can acknowledge our limits, while striving forward to learn and grow. It also frees us to ask for help or hire the right people to fill the gap—rather than exhausting ourselves trying to do something we were never meant to do alone. Facing the truth gives us the power to change it.

A Story of Growth

Take Sam, a small business owner struggling to manage his staff. He often found himself blaming external factors for employee turnover, telling himself it was the market or the staff's lack of commitment. But after some hard truths from a mentor, Sam realized his leadership style lacked clarity and empathy.

Initially hurt by the critique, Sam decided to observe his behavior and seek knowledge on the training needs of his team. Over time, he implemented changes, and his relationships improved. Employees became engaged in the process and the company bringing better performance and helping the company grow. The storm that had shaken his business became the catalyst for personal and professional transformation.

Plan for Storms

Planning for storms means preparing for the inevitable, or unforeseen challenges that arise on any journey. Storms can alter our path, disrupt our expectations, and even cause us to question our direction. However, they also hold the potential for discovery, growth, and sometimes, an entirely new and better destination. When storms come, they may change the landscape entirely. This is where you decide: will you use your compass to get back on the original course, or will you embrace the storm's lesson and adjust to a new direction? Either way, you remain in control as the navigator of your journey.

The Insight Storms Bring

Storms often challenge our assumptions and force us to reevaluate what truly matters. They can expose what we've ignored, shine a spotlight on hidden opportunities or on the weaknesses we need to address. Like Columbus, who landed on a new shore by accident, storms can lead to discoveries far greater than what we originally imagined.

As we keep walking this goal journey, both internal and external storms will come. When they do, it's time to flip the script. The stories we tell ourselves in those moments hold power. Will we let them anchor us to discouragement? Or will we rewrite them to unlock new strength? That internal dialogue matters! The truth is, the negative version is often the lie. "I failed, so I must not be good enough" feels real, but it's not truth—it's just fear in disguise.

We can turn disaster into momentum. We can take a setback and use it as the very launchpad to move forward. Remember that mixed bag I talked about? Life's rarely all good or all bad. There's power in saying, "Yes, getting fired hurt—financially and emotionally. But now I'm choosing to build new skills, or launch that business I've always dreamed of." That shift changes everything.

Now, let's pause and be honest. There are truly painful—and even traumatic—experiences in life. Moments so heavy that just putting one foot in front of the other feels impossible. When the hurt is loud, raw, and all-consuming, it can feel like life has nothing good left to offer. I don't say that lightly, as I speak from experience. — seasons of so much pain that it was hard to breathe, let alone hope. Times when suffering seeped into every part of my world—my work, my friendships, my faith, my very sense of self.

You might be asking, "Where's the mixed bag in that?" And that's fair.

The truth is, sometimes the good in those moments isn't visible right away. Sometimes it doesn't show up until much later—after the pain has eased its grip and we've had time to recover. It's only in looking back that we spot the thread of growth woven through the ache, or the depth of compassion that suffering etched into our hearts.

We've all seen the contrast. Some people endure great pain and somehow, not only survive, but thrive. While others live with the aftershocks for years—the pain continuing to echo through every corner of their lives. Both paths are hard. Both require more strength than words can capture. But one leads to restoration, healing, and even joy—not because the pain disappears, but because we learn how to carry it differently.

Let's be real: how to deal with that kind of deep, soul-level struggle could be a whole book in itself—and maybe someday it will be. Because facing pain with honesty, and finding your way through it, is not just a part of the journey... it's a journey all its own. One that's worth taking.

The power? We choose. We choose how we view the circumstances and how we deal with it. The risk? That we sit in the circumstances, throwing up our hands and living as victims. The truth is our path, regardless of what it looks like, it is always in our power to choose. Do we get off the path that is right for us sometimes? Absolutely! Do we need a course correction? Absolutely. But our current circumstance does not make a permanent one.

Don't let it pass you by. Look for the insight that is tucked within what the storm brings. Seek out the blessing, the benefit, the opportunity—even when it's hidden beneath the wreckage. Let your perspective shift and stretch. Let it grow. Become the phoenix that rises—not just from the ashes, but from the weight of everything that once held you back. Cut the chains. Lift your wings. And learn to fly even when the storm still rages.

Steps to Navigate Storms

1. **Acknowledge the Storm**
   Recognize the challenge for what it is—a temporary disruption, not an insurmountable obstacle. Storms always pass.

2. **Reflect on the Landscape**
   Has the storm altered your original path, or revealed new possibilities? Evaluate whether to stay the course or adjust.

3. **Revisit the Compass**
   Use your original plan as a guide, but stay flexible. Remember that the destination can be reached through different routes.

4. **Seek Support**
   Don't be afraid to reach out to mentors, friends, or

professionals. A trusted navigator can help you see solutions you might miss.

5. **Replace Doubt with Truth**
   When doubt creeps in, examine its source. Write down a counter-truth to replace the false belief.

Your Storms and Next Steps

Reflection Questions:

- What storms have I encountered in the past, and how did I navigate them?

- Are there any potential storms I can anticipate now?

- What doubts or false beliefs might be holding me back?

- What truths can I use to counteract those doubts?

Storms are an inevitable part of life's journey. While they may knock us off course temporarily, they also hold the potential for transformation and discovery. By planning for storms and addressing their impact with courage and honesty, we not only reach our destination but also enrich our experience of the journey itself. That's our day-to-day existence. And that is powerful.

Step by Step

Embarking on a journey toward your goals is a process of progression. Just as you can't get from the East Coast to the West Coast without crossing the states in between, you can't reach your destination without traversing the steps that lead you there. Each part of the journey, no matter how small, holds value—it's where growth, learning, and discovery happen.

Plans can change when traveling. You might decide to take a northern route, a southern path, or even explore every state along the way. The key is understanding that movement is sequential—step by step. Progress may vary; some days you'll move quickly, while others may require slow, deliberate steps. The important part is to keep moving forward.

Step by step isn't just about motion—it's about mindset. It's the decision to take the next right action, even when the whole path isn't clear. It's choosing to show up, to try again, to do the small things that build big things over time. It's honoring the process instead of rushing the outcome.

The journey is the refining ground. You'll hit stretches that feel like smooth sailing—and others that feel like crawling through mud. But neither moment defines the whole. It's what you gain along the way—perseverance, insight, strength, clarity—that becomes part of who you are when you finally arrive. The goal matters, but so does who you become in the getting there.

And if you feel like you're barely inching forward right now—keep going. Tiny steps still cover ground. Forward is forward.

Every small movement matters—sometimes it's not about the size of the step, but the commitment to keep stepping.

Keep Your Feet Moving

Emmitt Smith, the legendary Dallas Cowboys running back, is a prime example of this principle in action. On the field, he faced towering walls of opponents determined to stop him. Yet, no matter what obstacles stood in his way—or how many tried to bring him down—his feet never stopped moving.

Smith's tenacity and ability to pivot, dodge, spin, and adapt made "impossible" plays and "impossible" yard gains possible. His relentless forward momentum carried him to the top, earning him a place as one of the greatest players in NFL history.

The lesson? Keep your feet moving, no matter what barriers stand in your way. Even if you have to shift, spin, or change direction— momentum matters more than perfection.

Focus on the Next Step

Uncertainty often holds us back. We can see Step A and we can see our vision at Z —but we can't see the path in between. The gap feels overwhelming even impossible. Sometimes it's that frustration that has us walking away. But here's the truth: you don't need the full map to take the next step.

There will be moments when you can only see one or two steps ahead, and the rest of the path seems shrouded in uncertainty. That's okay. During those times, focus on the step right in front of you. Whether it's a math problem, a tough decision, or a moment of doubt —doing the next right thing unlocks progress. That one step that you can see leads to the next... and then the next. Complete each step and then look for the next.

If the only visible step is asking for help, take it! Seeking advice or support is movement. Trust that as you keep moving, the path will begin to reveal itself.

When the view clears, you may realize that you've strayed slightly off course—and that's fine. It's a chance to adjust course.

Alternatively, you might discover an exciting new destination—one you hadn't even imagined when you started. Someone who sets out to complete a 2K charity walk may find themselves inspired to train for a full marathon.

Goals evolve as we journey toward them, and sometimes the detours become the most rewarding part of the trip.

Ready to Plan the Trip

Now that you've set your destination, prepared yourself for challenges, and gained insight into the "lay of the land," it's time to dive into the nitty-gritty of planning. Like any well-thought-out adventure, this part of the process ensures you're equipped to handle whatever comes your way.

Planning your journey involves laying the groundwork for success. It's about preparing for obstacles, aligning resources, and creating a roadmap to guide you. Remember, every journey is unique. Take what serves your purpose and leave behind what doesn't.

Here's what's ahead as we map out the trip plan:

- **Budget**: Allocating resources effectively to support your journey.

- **Travel Partners**: Choosing companions who will encourage and challenge you along the way.

- **Mode of Transportation**: Deciding how you'll navigate the journey (strategies and tools).

- **Accommodations**: Creating a supportive environment for rest and rejuvenation.

- **Research Activities/Things to Do**: Enhancing your experience by identifying opportunities for growth and enjoyment.

- **Automate Obligations/Bills**: Freeing mental space by reducing day-to-day burdens.

- **Minimize Travel Risks**: Planning contingencies for potential storms to keep your journey smooth.

- **Pack (Stack the Deck)**: Gathering the tools, skills, and resources you'll need to succeed.

With this plan in hand, we'll take the first steps toward making your goals a reality. Up next, we'll talk about the foundation of every journey: your **budget**. Whether it's financial, emotional, or time-based, knowing how to allocate your resources will set the stage for success.

Let's keep moving forward, one step at a time. The adventure continues!

Budget: Planning the Resources for Your Journey

A budget is a foundational element of any goal-setting journey. It's more than just financial planning—it's about allocating all resources, including time and energy, in a way that supports your success. Whether your goal is personal or business-related, creating a detailed and realistic budget will keep you organized, focused, and prepared for the challenges ahead.

Financial Budget: Planning for the Costs

Every goal comes with its own set of costs, which can include tangible expenses and hidden ones. Breaking these down into categories makes the budgeting process clearer and more actionable. Let's explore some common areas:

1. Personal Goal Example: Health and Fitness

If your goal is to get fit and healthy, your financial budget might include:

- **Workout Clothing**: Proper attire for comfort and performance.

- **Gym Membership**: Monthly or annual fees.

- **Equipment**: Items like yoga mats, weights, or a treadmill.

- **Classes or Trainers**: Online subscriptions, in-person training, or group fitness classes.

- **Nutrition**: Adjusting grocery costs for healthier food choices, meal prep services, or supplements.

- **Miscellaneous**: Unexpected costs, like replacing worn-out equipment or trying new activities.

2. Business Goal Example: Starting a Small Business

If your goal involves launching or growing a business, you might plan for:

- **Initial Setup Costs**: Business registration, licensing, or incorporation fees.

- **Tools and Technology**: Software subscriptions, equipment, or website hosting.

- **Marketing**: Social media ads, promotional materials, or branding costs.

- **Education and Training**: Courses, books, or certifications to enhance your skills.

- **Operational Costs**: Utilities, workspace rentals, or outsourced tasks (e.g., bookkeeping).

- **Contingency Fund**: Setting aside 10–20% of the total budget for unexpected expenses.

Budgeting Time: Your Most Precious Resource

Time is as valuable as money, if not more so. Success requires being intentional about how you allocate your hours. Here's how to budget your time effectively:

1. **Assess Current Time Usage**:

   o Track how you currently spend your days. Are there activities that can be reduced or eliminated?

   o Identify "time wasters" like excessive social media scrolling or unproductive habits.

2. **Prioritize Time for Goal-Related Activities**:

   o **Examples of Activities**: Training, planning, writing, coaching, exercise, skill-building, networking, or reflection.

   o Block out specific days or hours dedicated solely to your journey.

3. **Incorporate Flexibility**:

   o Life is unpredictable, so leave buffer times in your schedule to accommodate unexpected events or adjustments.

4. **Balance Commitments**:

    o Ensure you're still dedicating time to family, friends, and self-care. Neglecting these areas can derail progress by leading to burnout.

The Value of a Budget and Goal Tracker

Integrating a **budget tracker** with your **goal tracker** is a powerful way to stay organized and motivated. Here's why:

- **Visual Clarity**: Seeing your financial and time allocations side-by-side keeps you focused and aware of what resources are available.

- **Motivation**: Tracking progress toward both your goal and budget milestones reinforces the value of your efforts.

- **Adjustments**: Reviewing your tracker regularly helps you identify areas where you can optimize spending or time investment.

For example, if your fitness goal requires regular classes but your budget tracker shows overspending, you can adjust by substituting some classes with free online videos. Similarly, if you notice that time set aside for study is consistently being interrupted, you can reallocate that time to quieter periods.

＊＊＊＊＊＊＊＊＊＊＊＊＊＊

Budgeting for a business especially, take in depth planning and understanding of what expenses you will encounter, as well as realistic sales/income expectations. If you are already accomplished in finance, then you likely already have a good handle on what you need. However, many who start the process leave finances to the unknown or last aspect to be planned in reaching for their goals. The budget outline below is designed to get the thought processes started and not intended to be an in-depth budget plan.

Use this to get you started on the journey and develop it as needed based upon your specific goals.

Generalized Budget Plan

Here's a versatile template for budgeting that applies to most goals:

Financial Budget

Category	Estimated Cost
Tools/Equipment	$_____
Education/Training	$_____
Subscriptions/Memberships	$_____
Marketing/Networking	$_____
Operational Expenses	$_____
Miscellaneous/Contingency	$_____

Time Budget

Activity	Hours/Week
Skill Development	_____
Goal-Specific Tasks	_____
Research/Planning	_____
Self-Care/Rest	_____

Activity	Hours/Week
Family/Friends/Commitments	_____

Tips for Effective Budgeting

- **Write It Down**: Whether in your planner, a spreadsheet, or an app, recording your budget helps turn intentions into actions.

- **Review and Reflect**: Use tools like the *Embrace the Journey Planner* to analyze what worked well and what needs adjustment each month.

- **Start Small**: If your resources are limited, begin with low-cost or time-light options. Gradually increase investment as you progress.

- **Celebrate Budget Milestones**: Treat yourself when you stick to your financial or time budget—it keeps the process rewarding.

What Will Your Budget Look Like?

- **What is your total financial budget?**
  $_____

- **How much time will you dedicate weekly?**

- **What days/times will you block out for progress?**

Budgeting your resources is a crucial part of the planning process. Whether you're preparing for personal growth or professional success, having a clear financial and time plan sets you up for a smoother journey. Next, we'll move into selecting **Travel Partners** and other essentials to keep your journey both productive and enjoyable!

Travel Partners

Choosing who to share your journey with is one of the most critical steps in reaching your goals. The people we allow into our inner circle—our "travel partners"—have a direct influence on our experience. They can either uplift us, helping us soar higher, or drain our energy, pulling us away from our path. Some travel partners might walk with us for just a mile, while others may be with us for the entire journey . Regardless of their duration, the influence they have can shape the quality of our experience.

Before sharing your goals and dreams, it's essential to reflect on the people in your life. Who will encourage you? Who will celebrate your successes? Who will find joy in being part of your journey? And just as importantly, who might unintentionally (or intentionally) drain your momentum or sow seeds of doubt?

Positive Relationships: The Wind Beneath Your Wings

The people who positively impact our journey are often mentors, encouragers, cheerleaders, or fellow travelers. These individuals help us maintain focus, provide perspective, and lend a listening ear when challenges arise. They see the potential in us, even when we struggle to see it ourselves, and their belief can reignite our motivation during tough times.

Imagine sharing your vision with someone who truly gets it—someone who lights up when you talk about your goals and says, "I believe in you. How can I help?" Their excitement becomes fuel for your journey. These are the people who will remind you of your "why" when obstacles cloud your path. They'll share insights, point out opportunities you may have missed, and celebrate every step forward, no matter how small.

Examples of Positive Impact

- **Encouragement**: A friend who regularly checks in, cheering you on as you work towards your goal.

- **Insight**: A mentor who provides feedback that sharpens your approach and helps you avoid pitfalls.

- **Support**: A family member who takes on extra responsibilities to free up your time for the journey.

Remember, positivity doesn't mean uncritical agreement. Constructive criticism, delivered with kindness and a genuine desire to help, can be invaluable. We don't need people who blindly agree with us. What we need most are people who truly care about us and are willing to engage in authentic conversations even when they are difficult. Who opens our eyes to more than one way to look at things, and challenges our one view perspective? A true ally in your journey isn't afraid to challenge you when it's needed but does so in a way that builds you up, not tears you down.

As we grow, sometimes relationships shift in ways we didn't expect. When we first connect with someone, especially a mentor or a strong supporter, it often meets a deep need — for both sides. Maybe they saw a place where they could help guide us, and in doing so, it also fulfilled something for them. But as we find our footing, gain confidence, and even grow beyond the place where they first found us, it can change the dynamic. It's not uncommon for that shift to stir up some discomfort, sometimes without either person even realizing it.

It takes a real openness and emotional maturity — on both sides — to recognize when the relationship is evolving. A mentor who can step back and allow the relationship to grow into a deeper, more equal connection is a rare gift. And if we're ever in that mentor role ourselves, we owe it to the people we care about to do the same. It's an act of love to allow the relationship to move beyond one season into something richer and more lasting. When we choose to grow together, the rewards can be incredible.

But sometimes, despite our best efforts, it's okay to acknowledge that a relationship has run its course. I once had someone come into my life during a time when I was at a deep low. They offered encouragement, tangible help, and genuine care — and they walked with me for a season I'll always be grateful for. But as I began to find my path and regain my strength, things started to shift. I noticed irritation creeping into our interactions. Almost every conversation became a correction, as if anything different from their way of thinking needed to be adjusted. I don't believe they even realized it was happening.

The relationship eventually ended when I set a boundary — lovingly and respectfully — asking for space to live my own way without feeling constantly corrected. I expressed genuine gratitude for everything they had poured into my life, but made it clear that mutual respect was needed moving forward. They chose to step away. And yes, it stung at the time. But with distance, I can see it clearly: I'm still incredibly thankful for the role they played during that important chapter of my life.

Of course, there are also times when **we** are the ones who naturally drift away. Growth can lead us in different directions, and that's part of life too. Every relationship invites us to be intentional about where and with whom we invest our time.

That said, I would encourage you to recognize the deep rewards that come from relationships that last through seasons of growth and change. When we choose to honor and nurture connections — even as they evolve — we add richness and depth to our own lives. Long-lasting relationships may look different than they once did, but they can become something even greater: a true treasure shaped by time, growth, and mutual respect.

Negative Relationships: Anchors That Drag You Down

On the flip side, there are those whose presence can hinder your progress. These are individuals who project their own fears, insecurities, or negative experiences onto your journey. They may mean well, but their doubts, criticisms, or pessimism can erode your confidence and momentum.

Some people only see in you the potential for failure and disappointment. Others may subtly (or overtly) dismiss your dreams as unrealistic or unimportant. Still others may constantly shift conversations back to themselves, unable or unwilling to support you in your endeavors.

It's important to have a game plan for these relationship moments. Preset actions or responses that will protect you from the negative results that tend to accompany these types of interactions. If confrontation, or boundaries are difficult for you, it's even more critical to preset in your own mind what your responses will be. Make a rule for yourself, so that when the moment comes you do not allow yourself to be intimidated or influenced negatively.

Strategies for Insulating Yourself

1. **Set Boundaries**: You don't have to cut these individuals out of your life, but you can limit how much you share about your goals with them. You can also not engage if they bring it up or want to discuss it with you.

   In my marriage, I was working to eat healthy and address my view about my weight. My husband, who on the surface would say he wanted that for me as well, would go out of his way to bring home my favorite sugary treats. Whether consciously or subconsciously, he was sabotaging my goals. I in turn had to choose how to deal with that.

   We can't control others, so the only person I could control was myself. At various times, I might change strategies such as mentioning it and then throwing the items away or giving them away. Or, deciding before it occurred, that I would not engage or eat anything he brought home. It was not just with someone else I had to set boundaries, but with myself as well.

   In business, there will be many around you who will tell you that it can't be done. They'll come up with all the reasons you, or the business, will fail. The reasons ultimately won't matter to the process of you reaching your goals. Some people you may disengage from communicating with, but others we may not be able to avoid.

At times, it may be impactful to speak up and ask someone to cease giving their opinions. You can take the objections and look them full in the face. If those objections are legitimate then look at them like an opportunity to overcome them before they are issues.

Remember, there is more than one way to get to your destination. Many times, the road will look different than we expect it to. Find the "how" not the "if". Treat them as if they were coming from a friend in a way that allows you to use it for a better outcome for yourself and then let the rest go. And if someone is overwhelming you with their negativity, then don't hesitate to create space from that person.

2. **Reframe Their Input**: Recognize that their negativity often reflects their own fears or experiences, not the reality of your journey.

   People relate from their own experiences. It's natural. It takes true emotional maturity to look past our own frame of reference to engage in what's going on for someone else. It may sound cliché, but it is true that "broken people hurt people". So, the "negative nellies" you may encounter are really viewing it from their own limited perspective. If you know they are well intentioned, just thank them for caring enough to share their opinion and move on.

   You can recognize their good intention without buying into the message.

3. **Choose Not to Be Influenced**: Many things are a choice. The choice may be between two uncomfortable options, but it is still a choice.

   It might be difficult to hold boundaries or limit our time with people who have held prominent roles in our lives.

Instead, surround yourself with enough positive voices that the negative ones lose their power.

It is true that we become an average of the 5 people we hang around the most. Whether we like it or not, we can be influenced, even subconsciously. So, work to keep the balance tipped towards those who are on your side. Your positive influences and supporters are priceless, and you should treat them as such.

But when you have a moment of hesitation or struggle, remind yourself of your untwisted truth: Your value is inherent, and others' doubts do not define your abilities or worth.

I want to stop here and recognize that following through on the strategies above aren't easy. We are wired for community and feel peer pressure strongly —even as adults. Sometimes, it is those closest to us that bring us the greatest discouragement.

It is crucial to feel that pain, work it through and let it go. Our response can push us to pursue our goals out of anger or defiance. But in that moment, we lose —even if we ultimately succeed at the goal.

A journey filled with anger or defiance takes something powerful, freeing and joyous —and turns it inward into pain. It's a pain that follows us and colors everything we do.

So while personal relationships can cause difficulty as we move towards our goals, it's important to take a breathe and work it through.

Use those strategies!

Recognizing Toxic Dynamics

If you find yourself in relationships that are emotionally or physically harmful, seeking professional guidance can be crucial. Toxic relationships—especially those that oscillate between moments of exhibiting care and then destructive behavior—can erode self-esteem and drain energy you need for your journey. Sometimes, walking away is the best act of self-love and self-respect you can take. I want to encourage you here to seek support and assistance if you are experiencing a toxic relationship.

The Power of Accountability Partners

An accountability partner is one of the most transformative travel partners you can have. This person doesn't just cheer you on—they hold you accountable, providing structure and motivation as you work towards your goals. They help you break down your goals into actionable steps, track your progress, and provide honest feedback.

Accountability partners are especially powerful because they create an external layer of responsibility. When you know someone is counting on you to report back, it's a natural motivator to take action—even on days when you don't feel like it. This is about ownership, not judgment. Accountability partners help you see what's working, identify what isn't, and brainstorm solutions to keep you moving forward.

Impacts of Accountability Partners

1. **Increased Focus**: Regular check-ins help you stay aligned with your priorities.

2. **Enhanced Problem-Solving**: Two heads are better than one, especially when tackling unexpected challenges.

3. **Consistent Momentum**: Knowing you'll have to report progress can push you through procrastination or self-doubt.

4. **Creative Energy**: Brainstorming with someone else often sparks new ideas or approaches you wouldn't have considered alone.

Types of Travel Partners

The people you travel with can play all kinds of roles, each bringing something special to the journey. When you take the time to recognize and nurture those relationships, it makes the experience more meaningful — and it directly fuels real growth, breakthroughs, and lasting results.

1. **Mentors**
   Mentors are guides who have walked a similar path and can share their wisdom and experience from their own journey. They offer perspective and insight, helping you to navigate challenges with confidence.

2. **Cheerleaders**
   These are the friends and family members who bring unrelenting positivity and encouragement. They may not offer practical advice, but their belief in you is a powerful motivator.

3. **Fellow Travelers**
   People who are pursuing similar goals can be invaluable. They understand your struggles because they're experiencing them too. Sharing the journey with others builds camaraderie and accountability.

4. **Coaches**

   A coach is like a personal trainer for your goals. They help you set realistic objectives, refine your strategy, and overcome obstacles. Coaches often provide tools and techniques that take your journey to the next level.

5. **Counselors**

   For deeper emotional or psychological challenges, a counselor can provide support and healing. They help you unpack past experiences or beliefs that may be holding you back, paving the way for personal growth.

Give and Take: The Heartbeat of Healthy Relationships

Healthy relationships thrive on reciprocity. Just as you lean on your travel partners for encouragement, support, and perspective, it's important to give back. This balance of give and take not only strengthens your bond with others, but also enriches the journey for everyone involved.

Being a supportive travel partner doesn't have to be complicated. Sometimes, it's as simple as sending a text message to say, "I believe in you," or listening when someone needs to talk through a challenge. Other times, it might mean offering practical help, like brainstorming solutions or sharing resources that can propel them forward.

When we show up for our travel partners, something really beautiful happens — the journey becomes richer, fuller, and a lot more rewarding. It's not just about what we get out of it; it's about what we build *together*. We create a positive feedback loop. Investing in others doesn't drain us — it actually multiplies the energy, inspiration, and momentum we all need to keep moving forward. The more we pour into these relationships, the more we realize that success isn't a solo adventure. It's a shared experience, and it's in that give-and-take where real magic happens.

There are so many simple, meaningful ways to strengthen these connections as we go. Little things, done consistently, can turn good partnerships into great ones. Whether it's celebrating wins, offering a listening ear, or sharing tools that could help someone grow, the effort we invest in each other keeps the momentum alive. Here are a few ways you can keep expanding that spirit of give-and-take along the way:

Expanding the Give and Take

- **Celebrating Together**: Be sure to celebrate others' victories, no matter how big or small. No qualifications, no minimizing, no "yes, but" they have so far to go…. Instead of jealousy or resentment, embrace their success and celebrate their milestones with them. Recognizing someone else's progress creates a spirit of encouragement that flows both ways.

- **Listening Actively**: Sometimes, people just need a sounding board. Many of us when we hear someone we care about or are invested in pose a problem, we want to fix it. However, many times, sharing of their struggle or problem isn't necessarily asking for solutions. They need to verbally work it through for themselves. Talking can help them release negative thoughts or emotions that are holding them back and it isn't necessarily something to be fixed. Offering your undivided attention can be a powerful gift that fosters mutual respect.

- **Sharing Resources**: We're always stronger together. When you come across a book, article, or tool that could help your travel partner, share it. It's a simple way to step outside of ourselves and lift up the people around us, all while staying focused on our own goals. Those small acts of thoughtfulness can create a ripple effect that makes a real difference — not just for them, but for you too.

- **Providing Honest Feedback**: Constructive criticism, delivered with kindness, can help others see blind spots and grow. Being a supportive travel partner sometimes means having the courage to tell the truth. But, just as important, is making sure the other person is open to hearing it. If they ask for feedback or bring a problem to you, that's your green light. If not, it's always better to ask first — something simple like, "Would you like my perspective?" Jumping straight into what you think they're doing wrong can shut someone down faster than it helps them. And when you do share, remember to hold it with an open hand — no strings attached. Both inwardly and outwardly, give them the grace and freedom to take what resonates and leave the rest. One of my favorite reminders is, *"Take from what I've shared and use what works for you, and dismiss the rest — no offense taken."*

As you invest in others, remember that balance is key. If you find yourself giving more than you receive, it may be time to reevaluate the relationship. Healthy partnerships are built on mutual respect, and both parties should feel valued and supported.

Protecting Your Focus: The Power of Boundaries

Your time, energy, and attention are among your most valuable resources. Protecting them is not about being selfish—it's about honoring your goals and ensuring that you can show up fully for yourself and others. Setting boundaries with family, friends, co-workers, and even yourself is an essential part of staying on course.

Holding Boundaries: A Real Act of Love

Boundaries can feel uncomfortable at first—sometimes, even downright awkward—especially when it comes to people we care deeply about. It's easy to fall into thinking that if we set a boundary we're somehow rejecting or hurting someone. But the truth is, setting healthy limits is one of the most loving things you can do. Not just for yourself, but for the people around you too.

Boundaries help you show up authentically. They protect your focus, your energy, and your peace. They reduce misunderstandings and resentment because they make your priorities clear. They create space where respect and trust can grow, instead of frustration or burnout creeping in quietly over time.

Setting boundaries doesn't mean slamming doors shut. It's more like opening a door, standing in it calmly, and saying, "Hey, I love you. I care about you. And I also need to care about this important part of my life right now."

Let's be real though—in the beginning, it can feel awkward or even selfish. It takes practice to get comfortable with it, and sometimes you'll second-guess yourself. That's normal. Keep going anyway. Each time you honor your needs *and* communicate with kindness, it gets easier.

Here are some examples of what holding boundaries can *actually* look like when you're in the middle of real life:

Practical Ways to Set Boundaries (and What They Might Sound Like)

With Family:
Family members often assume they have unlimited access to your time and energy. Not because they're trying to be disrespectful—but simply because that's how family often works!
When you're working toward a goal, it's important to communicate ahead of time what you'll need. You might say, "I'm working toward [goal], and I'll need some focused time each day to make it happen. I'm setting aside [time] for family, and I'd love to really be present with you then. But outside of that, I'll need space to work."

And when interruptions happen (because they will), you can gently remind them: "I love you, and I'll be able to focus so much better on us when it's our set time. Right now, I really need to stay focused on [project]. Thank you for understanding."

It's not cold. It's clear. And clarity is kindness.

With Friends:
Friendships thrive on honesty. Good friends want you to succeed, even if it means adjusting how you spend time together.

When invitations come up that conflict with your focus, you don't have to ghost people or make flimsy excuses. You can be real: "I would love to hang out, but I've promised myself to stick to my [workout plan, writing project, business building] right now. Can we find a time [next week, after this project wraps] when I can really be present and not distracted?"

You're honoring the friendship by being honest, not just showing up half-heartedly out of obligation.

With Co-Workers:

Boundaries at work can feel especially tricky because there's often an added pressure to be "team players." But being a good teammate doesn't mean abandoning your own responsibilities or goals.

If someone continually pulls you off track with their needs or emergencies, practice saying: "I hear you and I want to help, but I'm currently working under a tight deadline. Can we schedule a time to work through this later today or tomorrow?"

Or if you need to be more firm: "I'm committed to delivering [project] on time, so I need to stay focused. I'll circle back with you when I'm done."

Notice it's not rude. It's respectful—to them *and* to your own commitments.

With Yourself:

Let's not forget: some of the hardest boundaries to hold are the ones you set with yourself.

It's easy to blame external distractions, but sometimes the greatest threat to your journey is internal—procrastination, perfectionism, and fear dressed up as "taking a break."

You can parent yourself kindly, but firmly:

"I'll scroll for 10 more minutes and then put my phone down."

"I'm setting a timer for 25 minutes of focused work and then I'll earn a real break."

"I don't need to feel motivated to do x, y, or z—I just need to start. Action creates motivation."

Self-boundaries aren't about being harsh. They're about treating your goals like they matter. Because they do.

＊ ＊ ＊ ＊ ＊ ＊ ＊ ＊ ＊ ＊ ＊ ＊ ＊ ＊

Boundaries are *not* walls to keep people out. They are bridges that show others how to love and respect you well. They are commitments to yourself that say, "I believe in what I'm building."

You might feel resistance at first—from yourself and from others. That's okay. Resistance is normal whenever change happens. Stay kind, stay clear, and stay committed to your path.

Every time you hold a boundary, you're reminding yourself—and the people around you—that your dreams, your time, your energy, and your health are worthy of protection.

And that's not selfish.
That's growth.

Moving Forward: Preparing for the Journey Ahead

Before we dive into all the exciting ways to move forward, let's hit pause for just a second and really think about *who* and *what* you're bringing with you on this journey.

Because no matter how strong you are, no one does their best work in total isolation. We all need people and resources that fill our tank, lift our spirits, and remind us why we started in the first place.

Take a few moments to check in with yourself and ask:

- **Who are the people you want alongside you on this adventure?** (Not just anyone—choose the ones who make you braver, stronger, and more yourself.)

- **Who inspires you to keep growing, challenges you in all the right ways, and cheers for you even when things get messy?**

- **And maybe most importantly—how can *you* show up as that kind of person for someone else?**

Your answers to these questions are more important than you might think. They're not just about feeling good—they're about building a strong, steady community that helps you stay the course when the road gets bumpy.

These are your travel partners. Your people. The ones who will help you laugh through the hard parts, dance through the wins, and stay grounded in what matters most.

Now that your team is forming and your heart's in the right place, let's start talking about the practical side of the journey. Because dreams don't move themselves forward—you need a way to get from where you are now to where you're meant to go.

Transportation: Mapping Your Journey

How are you actually going to get from Point A to Point B? Your "transportation" represents the tools, methods, and pathways that will carry you toward your goals.

Just like picking the right vehicle for a road trip (sports car, minivan, motorcycle, sturdy old truck—whatever fits!), choosing your transportation for this journey will depend on your resources, your preferences, and the kind of adventure you're setting out on.

Let's dig into what that really looks like—and how to make smart, soul-aligned choices that actually get you where you want to go.

Defining Your Transportation: The Journey's Backbone

Your mode of transportation can take many forms, depending on the goal you're pursuing:

- **Education and Training**: If you're seeking a career change, promotion, or personal growth, education might be your transportation. This could include earning a degree, obtaining certifications, taking online courses, or attending workshops and seminars.

- o *Example*: Imagine someone who wants to transition from being a teacher to working in instructional design. Their "transportation" might include completing an online course in instructional design, attending industry webinars, and networking with professionals in the field.

- **Fitness Goals**: If your destination is improved fitness or health, your transportation could include gym memberships, yoga classes, running clubs, or even at-home workout routines.

  - o *Example*: A person working toward running a marathon might combine strength training at the gym, long-distance runs on weekends, and swimming to improve endurance.

- **Creative Pursuits**: For those chasing artistic or creative goals, transportation might include attending art classes, participating in writing workshops, or joining a community of like-minded creators.

  - o *Example*: A budding photographer might invest in online courses, shadow experienced photographers, and dedicate time to practice new techniques.

- **Professional Development**: For entrepreneurs, business leaders, or those growing a company, transportation might be a mix of mentorship, industry conferences, or hiring a coach to gain insight and direction.

  - o *Example*: A real estate agent expanding into luxury markets might attend high-end networking events, take specialized classes on luxury home marketing, and partner with a seasoned agent for mentorship.

Building Your Transportation System

Think of your journey like a train, with each car representing a crucial component of your transportation. Each car carries something essential, and together, they form a system that drives you toward your destination.

The Train Cars of Your Journey

- **Education Car**: Degrees, certifications, courses, or self-directed learning.

- **Mentorship Car**: Guidance from experienced individuals who can help you navigate your path.

- **Tools and Resources Car**: Equipment, software, or books necessary to support your journey.

- **Health and Wellness Car**: Nutrition, exercise, and self-care to maintain energy and focus.

- **Action Steps Car**: The tangible tasks and steps that propel you forward.

Each train car is critical, but not all will weigh the same. For some journeys, the mentorship car may be more significant than the education car. For others, tools and resources might take center stage. What matters is that each car is connected and moves you closer to your destination.

Here's the key: **Your transportation system isn't a one-size-fits-all setup.** It's uniquely yours, and it may look very different from someone else's—even if you're headed in the same general direction. Maybe you're relying heavily on that Action Steps car right now, tackling tasks and knocking things off the list, while your Education car is just quietly coasting along in the background. Or maybe you're in a season where your Health and Wellness car needs extra attention so you have the stamina to pull the rest of the train.

The beauty of this system is that you can *adjust* as you go. You're not locked into a rigid formula—you get to move the weight around, add new cars when you need them, or even park one temporarily at the station while you focus on another.

The most important thing? **Keep your train moving.** Check in with yourself regularly:

- Are all your cars still hitched together, or has something slipped off the track?

- Do you need to shift resources to strengthen a weaker link?

- Are you paying attention to the engine—the "why" behind your journey—that keeps the whole thing moving forward?

Remember, it's not about having the *perfect* setup. It's about building a system that works for *you*—one that's flexible, resilient, and aligned with where you're headed. When you take the time to intentionally shape your transportation system, you're not just drifting toward your goals—you're actively driving toward them with purpose, momentum, and heart.

Choosing Your Mode of Travel

Transportation isn't one-size-fits-all. It's about selecting the modes and methods that work best for you. While some steps may not excite you, embracing the journey means finding value and purpose even in the less thrilling parts.

Questions to Consider When Choosing Your Mode:

1. **What Inspires You?** If you're drawn to activities that spark joy or excitement, those will naturally be easier to sustain.

2. **What Are Your Non-Negotiables?** Identify the activities or tools that are essential for progress.

3. **What Fits Your Lifestyle?** Be realistic about your time, resources, and energy. If you hate running but love swimming, prioritize activities that align with your preferences.

4. **Who Can Support You?** Do you need a mentor, coach, or travel partner to help guide you?

Creating the Experience of the Journey

Part of "embracing the journey" is shaping the experience itself. How do you want this journey to feel? Do you want it to be structured and methodical, or more flexible and exploratory? Your transportation choices will influence this experience.

- *Example*: If your goal is to learn a new skill, you might decide to take an online course at your own pace, offering flexibility. Alternatively, you might enroll in a formal class with deadlines and group projects for structure.

Final Questions for Reflection:

- What modes of transportation resonate with me the most for this goal?

- What "train cars" (education, mentorship, tools, etc.) are essential for my journey?

- How can I shape my journey to make it enjoyable and sustainable?

- What resources do I need to begin moving forward?

- Who or what can help me stay on track?

Let these questions guide you as you prepare your transportation. Once your train is on the tracks, there's no stopping the momentum you'll build as you embrace your journey.

Accommodations: Creating Your Environment for Success and Rest

When planning any journey, the accommodations you choose are your sanctuary—a home base from which you launch your activities and return to rest and recharge. In the same way, as you embark on the journey toward your goals, your "accommodations" represent the intentional spaces, habits, and moments of self-care you set aside to rejuvenate and refocus. These are essential for sustaining the energy and motivation needed to keep moving forward.

Accommodations aren't just about convenience; they're about creating a nurturing environment where you can thrive. They provide comfort, safety, shelter, and rest—all vital for weathering the challenges and distractions along the way. Neglecting this aspect of your journey can lead to burnout, frustration, and even abandoning your goals altogether.

The more you can pre-decide or automate, the less mental and emotional energy gets drained on things that don't actually move you toward your goals. It's not just about staying organized—it's about protecting your focus and your fuel. Basic things like nutrition and hydration are massive when it comes to keeping your energy up, but they're also easy to let slide when life gets full. That's why it's worth taking time to decide—*in advance*—what your go-to solutions will be when your plate is full. Maybe that's stocking pre-made meals in the fridge, asking your spouse or a family member to pitch in more during busy seasons, or simply carrying a water bottle as a non-negotiable part of your day. Little systems like this don't just make life easier—they free up your capacity to stay present and productive. And no, it's not about perfection. Life will still happen. Things will fall through. But creating a general setup—a reliable default you can return to—gives you a stable foundation that can weather the chaos.

Take for example, the mom who's juggling work, college, and parenting. Her goals are huge and meaningful, but without accommodations that support them, burnout is almost guaranteed. That might mean calling in reinforcements—leaning on her husband or her mom to help with household responsibilities, child care, or the daily life logistics that can quietly chip away at study time or mental clarity. Something as simple as putting bills on auto-pay can lift a surprising amount of weight. These small shifts add up. They carve out the breathing room to think, to rest, and to stay aligned. And that rest? It's not optional. Carving out time to replenish your energy isn't selfish—it's what allows you to show up fully for both your goals and the people you love. Whether you're in study mode, family mode, or goal mode, having a nurturing environment to return to makes all the difference in how far—and how well—you go.

The Cost of Neglecting Rest

Many of us underestimate the importance of accommodations in our personal and professional lives. We push ourselves hard, thinking rest is a luxury we can't afford. But the truth is, rest is not a weakness—it's a strength. Failing to prioritize self-care often results in hitting a breaking point, where even the simplest tasks feel insurmountable.

For example, someone juggling full-time work, family responsibilities, education, and community commitments without ever taking time to breathe. Without intentional rest and reflection, this person is running on empty, unable to give their best to their responsibilities or themselves. Eventually, the fallout will come—in health, relationships, and performance.

Learning to value rest and self-care is a vital part of the journey. It's not a sign of failure; it's a sign of growth. Just like when learning to walk, falling down teaches us how to rise again and move forward stronger. Accommodations are the supportive structures we build to make it easier to get back up when we stumble.

What Do Accommodations Look Like?

Accommodations are personal to each individual, but they share the common goal of replenishing energy and maintaining focus. These can take many forms, depending on what brings you comfort and joy.

- **Daily Rituals**: A quiet morning routine with coffee and prayer, a meditation session, or journaling time can set a positive tone for the day.

- **Physical Environment**: Creating a clean, organized, and peaceful space to work or rest can significantly reduce stress. This might mean decluttering your workspace, hiring help for household chores, or designating a specific area as your retreat.

- **Scheduled Downtime**: Plan regular breaks to recharge—whether that's a daily walk, a round of golf, or a weekend getaway to the countryside. These moments give you space to breathe and refocus.

- **Active Rest**: Activities like yoga, painting, gardening, or hiking can rejuvenate your mind and body while also providing joy and satisfaction.

- **Community Support**: Enlist the help of family or friends to share the load. For instance, getting everyone on board with household chores can free up time and mental energy for your goals.

Designing Your Accommodations

Just as hotels offer more than just a bed—fitness centers, pools, cafes, and room service—your accommodations for this journey should address multiple aspects of your well-being. Consider your physical, emotional, and mental needs when planning your rest stops along the way.

Ask Yourself:

- What makes me feel safe and comfortable?

- What brings me joy and refreshes my spirit?

- How can I design my environment to reduce stress and encourage focus?

- Who can I rely on for support?

The Importance of Planning Ahead

One of the most powerful aspects of accommodations is their ability to provide support during difficult moments. By planning ahead, you ensure that your environment is ready to sustain you even when challenges arise.

For example:

- **Household Organization**: Work with your family to delegate chores and responsibilities. When everyone understands the plan, you can minimize conflicts and distractions.

- **Decision Fatigue**: Pre-plan your accommodations so that in moments of stress, you don't have to make decisions on the fly. Whether it's scheduling time for a massage or having healthy meals prepped, having these things in place reduces the mental load during tough times.

Remember, accommodations are not optional if you want to enjoy the journey. They are essential for maintaining momentum and ensuring that setbacks don't derail your progress.

Moving Forward

With your accommodations in place, you are setting yourself up for a more enjoyable and sustainable journey. Next, it's time to explore the activities that will help you make the most of your adventure. Just as a trip to Disney World includes planning which rides and attractions to visit, your journey to success involves planning the activities that will directly move you toward your goal.

Reflective Questions

- What accommodations do I need to set up to support my journey?

- What brings me comfort, joy, and rest?

- How can I create a nurturing environment that sustains me through challenges?

- Who can I rely on to share the load or help reduce stress?

Take time to reflect and plan your accommodations with care. Your success depends not just on the steps you take but also on the support you create for yourself along the way.

Research Activities: Curating the Experiences That Move You Forward

Planning a journey is more than just picking a destination and charting a route; it's also about choosing the activities along the way that will enrich your experience and propel you toward your goals. Think of these as the landmarks, rest stops, and excursions that make the trip not only worthwhile but enjoyable and memorable. Similarly, in the journey toward your goals, the activities you choose to engage in can enhance your progress, deepen your learning, and sustain your motivation.

Designing the Activities That Serve Your Goal

When planning your journey, identify the activities that will contribute directly to reaching your destination. These could range from attending classes or workshops, joining professional networks, engaging in physical training, reading industry literature, or dedicating time to skill-building exercises. The key is to ensure that these activities align with your big-picture goals and provide a clear benefit to your progress.

Preparing for a Marathon

If your goal is to run a marathon, your research activities might include:

- Developing a training schedule for daily runs.

- Learning about nutrition for endurance athletes.

- Investing in proper running gear.

- Scheduling time for strength training or yoga to build overall stamina.

- Connecting with local running groups for support and accountability.

Imagine discovering a local park with a challenging trail you've never explored before. Taking a run there not only diversifies your training, but also keeps the process interesting and fun. This could even become a regular part of your routine if it adds value and enjoyment to the experience.

Advancing in Your Career

If your goal is to gain a professional designation, your activities might include:

- Registering for online courses or in-person classes.

- Creating a study schedule and planning for exam dates.

- Networking with professionals who have already achieved the designation.

- Attending industry seminars or webinars to deepen your knowledge.

Picture this: during a networking event, you meet someone who offers to mentor you. This unexpected opportunity becomes a cornerstone of your journey, providing insights and guidance that accelerate your progress.

The Power of Saying "Yes" and "No"

Not all opportunities that come your way will serve your purpose. Knowing when to say "yes" and when to say "no" is critical to staying on course.

Learning to Say "Yes"
Sometimes, the most unexpected opportunities can add tremendous value to your journey. For example:

- A friend invites you on a challenging hike while you're training for a marathon. This activity complements your goal while offering the added benefits of variety and social connection.

- You're introduced to a "guru" in your field who offers mentorship. This unplanned relationship could provide insights and opportunities you hadn't considered.

Learning to Say "No"
Other times, distractions can masquerade as opportunities. It's essential to evaluate whether an activity aligns with your goal or merely takes time away from it. For example:

- You're preparing for a major test, and a friend invites you to a late-night movie. While tempting, this might leave you tired and unfocused the next day, potentially jeopardizing your performance.

However, saying "no" doesn't have to mean shutting yourself off from enjoyment or connection. Perhaps you decide to catch an earlier showing or postpone until after your test. This way, you strike a balance between honoring your goal and nurturing your relationships.

Balancing Preplanned and Spontaneous Activities

While planning your activities, leave room for spontaneity. Some of the most enriching experiences are the ones we don't anticipate. A chance encounter, an unexpected invitation, or a serendipitous discovery can all add value to your journey if they align with your purpose.

At the same time, maintaining a clear focus on your ultimate goal ensures that you stay on track. Regularly reflect on your activities and ask yourself:

- Does this serve my goal or purpose?

- Is this activity enhancing my journey or creating unnecessary detours?

- How can I adapt this opportunity to align with my overall objectives?

Creating Your Activity Plan

To keep track of your activities and ensure they align with your goal, consider using a planner or goal tracker. A budget tracker for both time and money can help you allocate resources effectively. Break down your activities into manageable steps, assigning deadlines or milestones to measure your progress.

Here's a general framework to guide your planning:

Step 1: Identify Core Activities

List the activities that directly contribute to your goal.

- What are the skills, knowledge, or experiences you need to achieve your objective?

- What resources or tools will you require?

Step 2: Explore Complementary Opportunities

Look for additional activities that enhance your journey.

- Are there workshops, events, or social groups that align with your goal?

- Are there new skills or experiences that could enrich your process?

Step 3: Evaluate and Prioritize

Ask yourself:

- How does this activity serve my purpose?

- What is the cost (time, money, energy) of this activity, and is it worth the investment?

- Will this activity bring joy, variety, or balance to my journey?

Step 4: Schedule and Reflect

Set aside dedicated time for your planned activities and build in opportunities to review your progress. Regular reflection will help you determine what's working, what isn't, and where you might need to adapt.

Reflective Questions

- What activities will directly further my goal?

- What unexpected opportunities might add value to my journey?

- How will I evaluate whether an activity aligns with my purpose?

- What tools (planner, tracker, mentor) can I use to organize and prioritize my activities?

By thoughtfully planning and reflecting on your activities, you create a dynamic and fulfilling journey. The next step is to explore how automating obligations can free up even more time and energy to focus on what truly matters.

Automate Obligations: Simplify, Streamline, and Sustain Your Journey

Reaching your goal requires focus, energy, and dedication—valuable resources that are often pulled in many directions by life's obligations. From household responsibilities to professional demands, our "to-do" lists can feel endless. The good news is that many of these tasks can be automated, outsourced, or adjusted to give you the bandwidth to focus on your journey. This isn't about shirking responsibilities; it's about being intentional with your time and energy so you can invest them where they matter most.

The Power of Automation

Automation is a powerful tool for freeing mental space and time. It allows you to set tasks in motion without requiring constant attention, creating room to concentrate on what truly propels you forward.

Automate Household Responsibilities

Start by looking at recurring household tasks.

- **Bills:** Put utilities, credit cards, subscriptions, and other regular payments on autopay to avoid missing deadlines and free up mental space.

- **Shopping:** Schedule deliveries for pet supplies, groceries, or household essentials through online services. This saves time and reduces the need for frequent store visits.

- **Cleaning:** Consider hiring a cleaning service, even just once a month, to lighten the load. Alternatively, set up a rotating schedule for family members to share household chores.

- **Meal Planning:** Invest time in creating a weekly or monthly meal plan. Prep meals in advance or use meal delivery services for convenience. Batch cooking and freezing homemade meals can save hours each week.

Automate Professional Obligations

Automation isn't just for household tasks; it's also a game-changer in professional settings.

- **Emails and Scheduling:** Use tools like auto-responders, scheduling apps, and shared calendars to streamline communication and time management.

- **Social Media:** Plan and schedule posts using platforms like SLMP (StreamLine Marketing Pro), Buffer or Hootsuite. This ensures your online presence remains active without daily effort.

- **Bookkeeping:** Employ software like QuickBooks or hire a virtual assistant to manage invoices and track expenses.

- **CRM Services:** Customer Relationship Management (CRM) systems like StreamLine Marketing Pro (SLMP), Salesforce, HubSpot, or Zoho can help you manage client interactions, streamline workflows, and keep track of important communications and deadlines.

Outsourcing: When to Let Someone Else Handle It

For tasks that can't be automated, outsourcing can be a smart solution. This doesn't mean admitting defeat—it means acknowledging where your time is best spent.

Household Examples:

- Hire a landscaper for lawn care.

- Use a laundry service or delegate laundry duties to family members.

- Pay for errand services to handle tasks like dry cleaning pickups.

Professional Examples:

- Bring in a virtual assistant to manage administrative duties.

- Outsource content creation or graphic design if it's not your strong suit.

- Partner with a marketing agency to handle outreach and campaigns.

Outsourcing doesn't have to be permanent. Consider it a temporary investment during the busiest phases of your journey.

Automating Your Schedule

Your time is one of your most valuable resources. Automating your schedule involves intentionally setting and protecting blocks of time dedicated to your goals.

Preset Time Blocks for Success

Set non-negotiable time slots in your calendar for tasks related to your journey. This might include training, studying, coaching sessions, or even self-care. Treat these blocks as sacred—commitments to yourself that take priority over less important distractions.

Maximize Your Time

- **Multitask Purposefully:** Listen to audiobooks or podcasts related to your goals during your commute or workouts.

- **Combine Activities:** Spend quality time with family while incorporating fitness goals, like playing soccer with your kids or going for a bike ride together.

- **Batch Tasks:** Group similar tasks together to maximize efficiency, such as meal prepping for the week or answering emails in designated time blocks.

Automating Accommodations

Accommodations are your personal oasis—a safe and rejuvenating environment that fuels your energy and enthusiasm. Automating your accommodations ensures they remain a priority even when life gets hectic.

Preset Rest and Relaxation

- Block off specific times in your schedule for unwinding. Whether it's a daily yoga session, a nightly reading ritual, or a monthly weekend getaway, commit to these moments as you would any other important appointment.

- Use alarms, reminders, or apps to reinforce habits like bedtime routines or meditation sessions.

Delegate or Simplify Where Possible

- If cleaning your home adds stress, hire help or set a family cleaning schedule.

- Create a designated space for reflection or relaxation, like a cozy reading nook or a meditation corner, and keep it maintained.

Establish Boundaries

Establishing and maintaining boundaries can be one of the most difficult things in our day to day lives regardless of whether we are reaching for a specific goal. There have been whole books written just on this subject alone. None of us wants to feel like "the bad guy". We may want to present a certain view for others to see that can be affected when we hold healthy boundaries. Women especially can feel a need to meet everyone else's needs before their own as we feel the "shoulds" stronger than most. We "should" be able to juggle it all – home, work, husband, kids, parents, siblings, colleagues, friends, etc. on top of home responsibilities such as cleaning, errands, groceries, cooking, bill paying, and more.

Sometimes boundaries can seem like the hardest thing in our lives to do. We may be pushing against our own learned behavior or even our nurturing instincts. Deciding ahead of time what these are going to look like is the first step. Our view can change with emotion or pressure, so setting this when we are in a place of peace and reason is important to success.

If this is an area in which you particularly struggle, then I recommend a mentor, accountability partner, or even counseling to work on this aspect specifically. This can be challenging, but is crucial to sustaining your focus and progress.

Here are some simple tactics to give you an idea of what some boundaries might look like for you. Remember, your journey is unique so what you need, and your specific boundaries, won't look like anyone else's.

With Family and Friends

- Explain your goals and ask for their support. Let them know how much their encouragement means to you.

- Set limits on social engagements that don't align with your goals. Politely decline or suggest alternative plans that work better with your schedule.

- Designate "quiet hours" when you won't be interrupted so you can focus on what moves you forward.

With Colleagues and Work

- Use shared calendars to indicate when you're unavailable for meetings or calls.

- Communicate clearly about deadlines and responsibilities to avoid last-minute demands.

- Delegate tasks when possible to ensure your workload is manageable.

Setting boundaries isn't about being selfish—it's about being intentional. When you protect your time and energy, you can show up more fully for both yourself and others.

Creating an Automated and Balanced Life

Automating obligations is more than just a productivity hack—it's a strategy for preserving the energy and focus needed to reach your goals. By reducing mental clutter and freeing up your schedule, you create space for creativity, growth, and meaningful progress.

Reflective Questions

- What tasks in my daily life can I automate or outsource?

- How can I streamline my schedule to make more time for my journey?

- What boundaries do I need to set to protect my time and energy?

- How can I ensure my accommodations for rest and rejuvenation remain a priority?

With your obligations handled, and your environment optimized, you'll be ready to tackle the challenges ahead. In the next section, we'll explore how to minimize travel risks and navigate potential pitfalls on your journey.

Minimize Travel Risk

Minimizing travel risk is about foreseeing potential challenges, obstacles, or "storms" that could derail the progress toward your goals. This proactive approach combines self-awareness, preparation, and strategic planning to create a smoother journey. By knowing the "lay of the land" and understanding your tendencies, weaknesses, and strengths, you can position yourself to overcome obstacles and maintain momentum.

Think of this as putting on a seatbelt before driving or carrying a first-aid kit on a hike. Preparation doesn't mean expecting failure—it means setting yourself up for success, no matter what comes your way.

Identify and Address Your Weaknesses

Understanding your weaknesses is a critical first step in minimizing risk. Self-awareness allows you to anticipate what might trip you up so you can take proactive measures. Whether it's a skill, personal character trait, or a habit that repeatedly derails your progress, naming it is powerful. Once you identify the areas that tend to hold you back—like procrastination, people-pleasing, disorganization, or overcommitting—you can put safeguards in place to reduce their impact.

Weaknesses can be a tender topic, especially when we're trying to grow. It's easy to fall into the trap of thinking we have to choose between self-acceptance and self-improvement—as if we're either "enough" as we are, or we're not measuring up. But that's a false choice. You can absolutely love who you are *and* want to become an even stronger, wiser, more effective version of yourself. Recognizing your weak spots doesn't mean you're failing—it means you're paying attention, and that's a powerful move.

As you start working on those areas—whether that means learning a new skill, shifting a mindset, setting better boundaries, or just being more honest with yourself—you'll often find it actually adds richness to the journey. What once felt like a liability can become a launching pad for growth. Some weaknesses are quick fixes, while others take a bit more time and intentionality to unpack. But the beauty is this: when you lean in, stay curious, and give yourself grace in the process, the journey becomes less about proving yourself and more about enjoying the ride, quirks and all.

The Organized Environment

While now I'm known for being organized and efficient, at one time organization was one of my greatest challenges. I find for myself, a clean and organized environment is essential to staying productive and focused. Clutter and disarray can create mental noise, making it hard to concentrate. I've learned to follow two simple rules:

1. **"A place for everything and everything in its place."** This rule minimizes the time and frustration of looking for misplaced items.

2. **Make tools accessible.** I keep cleaning supplies in easy-to-reach locations. As I move through the house, I can quickly clean or tidy without wasting time searching for what I need.

Your version of this might involve organizing your workspace, decluttering your digital files, or setting up a designated study or work area. When your environment supports your goals, you can focus your energy where it matters most.

Preplan Responses to Challenges

What are the obstacles you might face on your journey? Whether it's time constraints, competing obligations, or unexpected setbacks, having a plan in place can make all the difference.

Examples of Proactive Planning

- **Time Management:** If finding time to study is a challenge, schedule specific hours in advance. Block out these times as "non-negotiable" and communicate your commitment to those around you.

- **Family Coordination:** Create a separate space to work or study and coordinate with your partner or family members for support. For example, your spouse could manage the kids' bedtime routine while you use that time to focus on your goal.

- **Short-Term Sacrifices for Long-Term Gains:** Beth, a friend who pursued a medical degree, minimized her travel risk by balancing sacrifices. She spent less time with her children during her studies, but she also sacrificed a perfect GPA to ensure she maintained some family time. Her focus was on graduating and securing a fulfilling job in healthcare, not perfection.

Plan Ahead for Key Steps

Minimizing risk isn't just about solving problems—it's also about setting yourself up for success in future steps.

Examples of Forward Planning

- **Building Relationships:** If you'll need a professor's recommendation for admission to a program, start building rapport now. Volunteer for their projects, participate in discussions, and stand out in their classes.

- **Securing Resources:** Writing a book? Start searching for an editor or beta readers early so you're not scrambling at the last minute.

- **Financial Planning:** When I decided to pursue a psychology degree, I anticipated financial challenges and proactively traded my beloved Chevy Silverado Z71 for a more affordable option. This allowed me to fund my education without taking on loans.

Proactive planning like this minimizes the chance of being blindsided by foreseeable obstacles and ensures you're prepared to navigate the journey smoothly.

Embrace Self-Honesty

Looking at the road ahead requires honesty. It's tempting to see the journey through the lens of hope or good intentions, but an open, realistic view is essential for identifying potential risks.

Ask yourself:

- What events, circumstances, or people might pose challenges?

- What habits, weaknesses, or tendencies of your own could become obstacles?

- Are there ways to mitigate these risks now, before they grow into larger problems?

Minimizing risk means taking a grounded approach to your journey. It's not about expecting the worst; it's about being prepared so you can focus on the joy and fulfillment of reaching your destination.

Increasing Your Success Rate

Research shows that only about 8% of people successfully achieve their goals. By identifying and mitigating risks, you can significantly improve your odds. Each proactive step you take—whether it's budgeting time, securing resources, or setting boundaries—moves you closer to your goal and strengthens your resilience against setbacks.

Reflective Questions

- What risks or storms can you foresee on your journey?

- What actions can you take now to circumvent those challenges?

- How can you organize your environment, resources, or support system to minimize stress later?

With the right strategies in place, you'll be well-equipped to handle whatever challenges arise, keeping your focus on the road ahead. In the next section, we'll dive into "packing"—identifying exactly what you need to stack the deck and give yourself every possible advantage on your journey.

Packing

Packing is all about preparing yourself for success by gathering everything you need to stack the deck in your favor. It's about equipping yourself for the challenges and opportunities of the journey ahead. Depending on your destination and mode of travel, what you pack will be unique to you. And don't stress if you forget something—it's never too late to add what you need along the way. Let's break this process into categories and explore how you can pack for a fulfilling and successful journey.

Backpack/Suitcase

Your suitcase holds your tools—anything and everything that supports your journey. Think of this as your personal toolkit for success. These tools may be physical, digital, or even relational, depending on your goal.

For example:

- **Professional growth:** A planner, online courses, books, or software to streamline your tasks.
- **Fitness:** Proper workout gear, gym memberships, or a yoga mat.
- **Creative endeavors:** Art supplies, notebooks, or the latest version of your favorite editing software.

This category also includes items that keep you organized and on track. For instance, a robust planner can serve as both a tool and a guide for your journey. Digital tools like apps or task managers might also help you stay productive.

Actionable Step: Reflect on your goal and ask yourself: *What tools will make my journey smoother and more effective?*

Question:

- *What tools do I need to gather before I start?*
  _____
- *What would launch my goals forward and speed progress?*
  _____
- *What am I missing?* _____
- *How can I find, or move towards getting what I need?*
  _____

Sustenance (Fuel)

Fuel is critical for any journey. It's the physical, emotional, and mental energy you need to keep moving forward. Sustenance goes beyond food and water; it encompasses anything that refills your reserves and energizes you.

Physical Fuel:

- Plan meals or snacks that are nutritious and energy-boosting. Avoid items that drain you, such as processed foods or sugar-heavy treats. Instead, plan alternatives that you'll look forward to, like healthy protein snacks or smoothies.

Mental and Emotional Fuel:

- What fills your emotional tank? Perhaps it's listening to uplifting music, journaling, or taking a long walk in nature. Maybe it's reconnecting with your faith, spending time with family, or engaging in a creative hobby.

Practical Tips:

- Automate fuel when possible. For example, set up automatic deliveries for supplements or use meal-prep services to save time and energy.
- Schedule time for rejuvenation. If reading a book is what helps you reset, block out time in your planner for it. If yoga or meditation is your go-to, make it a non-negotiable part of your week.

Question:

- *What sustenance do I need to pack to fuel my journey?*

  _____

- *Is there anything draining my energy that I should avoid?*

  _____

Map

Before you set out, you need a map to give you direction. In the age of GPS, maps might seem outdated, but they're invaluable for seeing the big picture. Your map provides clarity, shows potential obstacles, and allows you to plan alternate routes.

Mapping your journey is about scheduling key milestones and breaking down your goal into actionable steps. For example:

- If you're pursuing a certification, map out deadlines for coursework, exam dates, and study hours.
- If you're launching a new business, your map might include a timeline for creating a business plan, securing funding, and marketing your services.

Use a Planner or Calendar:

Your planner isn't just a tool; it's part of your map. Schedule your steps, allocate time for each activity, and regularly review your progress. Time blocking is especially effective—it ensures that important tasks don't fall by the wayside.

Balance:

While mapping, leave space for flexibility. Life happens, and part of embracing the journey is being willing to adjust your course when unexpected opportunities or challenges arise.

Question:

- *What stops or milestones should I put on my map?*

_____

Compass

A compass helps you stay aligned with your values and purpose. It ensures that even when storms arise or you're tempted to stray, you remain on course.

Ask yourself:

- *Does my current path align with my values?*
- *Am I engaging in activities that serve my purpose?*

Your compass might also include people who guide you, such as mentors or accountability partners. They can help you reevaluate and reset when needed.

Actionable Tip: Keep your values visible—write them in your planner or display them somewhere prominent. This serves as a constant reminder of what's truly important. Values can easily disappear in both circumstances of success, or during struggle or stress.

Illumination

Illumination is about clarity—shedding light on the internal and external factors that might impact your journey.

Internal Illumination:

- What fears or self-limiting beliefs might hold you back? Are there doubts you need to address before moving forward?

External Illumination:

- Who or what in your environment might drain your energy or derail your progress?

By illuminating these areas, you can proactively address challenges. It's also about shining your light outward—helping and inspiring others along the way.

Questions:

- *What self-limiting beliefs are holding me back?*

  _____

- *What is a fear or uncertainty I hold about my goal?*

  _____

Emergency Beacon

An emergency beacon is your lifeline when things feel overwhelming or uncertain. This is where your support system comes in—those cheerleaders, accountability partners, and mentors who are there to help you stay the course.

How to Use Your Beacon:

- Verbalize your struggles. Sometimes, simply talking about a problem can reveal the solution.
- Seek guidance from those who've traveled a similar path. Their experience and perspective can provide clarity.
- Don't be afraid to ask for help. Relationships are one of the most powerful tools for overcoming challenges.

Failure

Failure can stop you completely, or you can use it as information for what to avoid next time. Asking questions like "why did it fail" can guide you into the next success moment. Failure is not the end of the journey—it's a lesson. Each misstep teaches you something valuable that brings you closer to your goal. In fact, let's get rid of that word "failure". It is now called "education" or "educational experience". No more failure! It's a lesson as you build your expertise, or take the next step on your journey. Embrace failure as part of the process and keep moving forward.

Questions:

- *Who will I reach out to when I need help?*

  _____

- *What lessons can I learn from past ~~failures~~/educational experiences?*

  _____

Reaching Your Destination

The journey doesn't end when you reach your goal. The destination is simply one part of a greater adventure. What matters most is the transformation that occurs along the way—the growth, the learning, and the experiences that shape who you are.

Once you've reached your destination, reflect on the journey. Celebrate your achievements and use what you've learned to dream up your next goal. Personal development is a continuous process, and every journey equips you with new tools for the road ahead.

Final Thought:
No matter what obstacles you face, nothing can stop your journey except you. Keep your feet moving, embrace every moment, and remember: you are unstoppable.

Questions:

- *What tools, sustenance, and resources do I need to pack for my journey?* _____

- *What self-limiting beliefs or fears need to be addressed before I start?*
  _____

- *Who are my top picks to journey with me, and how will I reach out to them?* _____

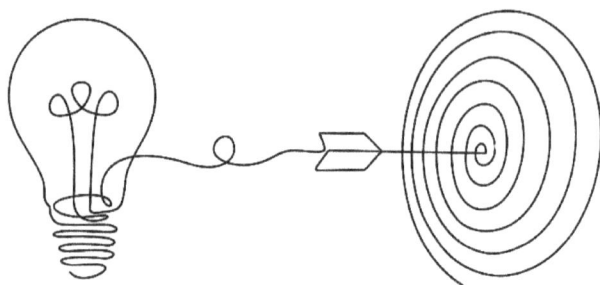

Part Two: Embrace the Journey – Turning Goals Into Action

Now that you've set the foundation for your journey, it's time to dive into actionable strategies that turn your aspirations into tangible accomplishments. Setting goals is only the beginning; the real work begins in the process of pursuing those goals step by step. This section focuses on understanding your unique work style, creating realistic plans, and staying flexible as you progress.

The **SMART method**, introduced by George T. Doran in 1981, provides a proven framework for creating goals that are clear, actionable, and achievable. Coupled with insights into your work style and personalized strategies, this method allows you to create a tailored plan for success.

Basics of Goal Setting

Goal setting is more than just deciding what you want to achieve; it's about building a roadmap to get there. Whether you aim to achieve a personal milestone, professional growth, or a creative endeavor, a well-defined goal provides clarity, purpose, and direction.

Define Your Goal

Every journey starts with a clear destination. Defining your goal ensures that you know exactly what you're working toward. If you're struggling to articulate your goal, revisit the first section of this book where we explored discovering your "why" and aligning your goals with your values.

Practical Example:

Instead of a vague goal like "get healthier," define it with clarity:

- *Specific:* "Lose 10 pounds through exercise and meal planning within three months."

- *Specific:* "Complete a half-marathon training program by December."

Ask yourself:

- What exactly do I want to achieve?

- Why does this goal matter to me?

Make It SMART

The SMART method takes your goal from idea to action by making it:

1. **Specific**: Define your goal with precision.
   - *Example:* Instead of "grow my business," say, "Gain five new clients by the end of the quarter."

2. **Measurable**: Track progress with clear metrics.
   - *Example:* "Save $5,000 in six months by putting aside $834 per month."

3. **Achievable**: Set a realistic yet challenging target.

   o   *Example:* "Write one chapter of my book each week," not "Finish the entire book in one week."

4. **Relevant**: Ensure your goal aligns with your values and long-term plans.

   o   *Example:* If financial freedom is a priority, focusing on savings or debt reduction may take precedence over taking an expensive vacation.

5. **Time-Bound**: Assign a deadline to create urgency and accountability.

   o   *Example:* "Launch my website by March 1st."

Break It Down and Prioritize

Big goals can feel daunting unless broken into manageable steps. Use the **Action Steps Worksheet** to organize your plan. This worksheet helps identify key steps and tasks, along with deadlines, to ensure steady progress.

How to Use the Worksheet:

1. Write down your goal at the top.

2. Identify major steps required to achieve it.

   o   *Example:* For a goal of writing a book:

      ▪   Step 1: Outline chapters.

      ▪   Step 2: Write one chapter per week.

      ▪   Step 3: Edit draft.

3. Break each step into tasks with deadlines.

   o *Example for Step 1:* Research themes, create chapter titles, and organize content ideas.

4. Regularly revisit and adjust your plan as needed.

Track Progress

Tracking your progress ensures that you stay on course and remain motivated. Set weekly and monthly benchmarks that align with your overall goal.

Weekly Tracking:

- Review tasks completed and plan the week ahead.

- Evaluate challenges and adjust strategies as needed.

Monthly Tracking:

- Set specific milestones to achieve each month.

- Example: If your goal is to learn Spanish, Month 1 might focus on vocabulary basics, Month 2 on grammar fundamentals, and so on.

This phased approach allows for flexibility and accommodates varying levels of effort across months.

Stay Flexible

Flexibility is a key component of long-term success. As life throws unexpected challenges your way, be willing to adjust your plan without abandoning your goal. In the first section of this book, we discussed how storms and detours can sometimes lead to new discoveries. Use these moments to re-evaluate your path and ensure it still aligns with your values and purpose.

Celebrate Success

Acknowledging your progress, no matter how small, is crucial for maintaining motivation. Reflect on milestones as victories that keep you energized for the journey ahead.

Examples of Celebrations:

- Reward yourself with something meaningful, like a dinner out or a day off.

- Share your accomplishments with supportive friends or family.

- Reflect on how far you've come and the lessons you've learned.

Understanding Your Workstyle

By understanding your unique strengths, weaknesses, and work styles, you can create a roadmap that reflects your individuality and propels you toward success. Keep building, adapting, and celebrating as you embrace your journey.

Your Work Style and Its Impact

Analytical Work Style

Characteristics: Detail-oriented, logical, data-driven, thrives on structure.

Effect on Goals –

> **Strengths:** Strong at creating detailed, step-by-step plans and tracking progress with measurable outcomes.
> **Challenges:** May overanalyze or delay action due to perfectionism.

Action Plan Tips:

- o Set clear, data-backed milestones with deadlines.
- o Use project management tools to track progress.
- o Incorporate regular check-ins to avoid analysis paralysis.

Creative Work Style

Characteristics: Big-picture thinker, imaginative, thrives on innovation.

Effect on Goals –

> **Strengths:** Great at brainstorming unique solutions and adapting to challenges.
> **Challenges:** May struggle with focus or consistency.

Action Plan Tips:

- o Break goals into smaller, manageable tasks with visual boards.
- o Build flexibility into your plan to accommodate inspiration-driven shifts.
- o Use creative rewards for achieving milestones.

Independent Work Style

Characteristics: Self-motivated, prefers autonomy, values freedom to make decisions.

Effect on Goals –

> **Strengths:** Strong at self-direction and staying disciplined without external oversight.

Challenges: May struggle with collaboration or accountability.
Action Plan Tips:
- o Use self-imposed deadlines and solo tracking tools.
- o Celebrate wins privately, but also share progress with a trusted accountability partner.
- o Plan for collaboration points to ensure balance.

Collaborative Work Style

Characteristics: Team-oriented, thrives in social settings, values input form others.
Effect on Goals –
    Strengths: Energized by group discussions and brainstorming, excels at leveraging collective resources.
    Challenges: May over-rely on others or get distracted by group dynamics.
Action Plan Tips:
- o Form accountability groups or goal-setting cohorts.
- o Regularly schedule team check-ins or updates to stay motivated.
- o Create solo tasks to balance dependence on others.

Pragmatic Work Style

Characteristics: Results-driven, focused on efficiency and outcomes.
Effect on Goals –
    Strengths: Highly efficient, skilled at prioritizing tasks for quick wins.
    Challenges: May neglect long-term planning in favor of immediate results.

Action Plan Tips:
- o Combine short-term wins with long-term objectives in your plan.
- o Use outcome-focused metrics to measure success.
- o Schedule time to reflect on progress and refine strategies.

Supportive Work Style

Characteristics: Empathetic, thrives on relationships and helping others.

Effect on Goals –

Strengths: Builds meaningful connections and excels in people-focused tasks.

Challenges: May prioritize others' goals over their own or hesitate to take risks.

Action Plan Tips:
- o Clearly define personal goals and boundaries.
- o Use goal-setting frameworks that prioritize both personal and team objectives.
- o Seek encouragement from mentors or peers for independent steps.

Spontaneous Work Style

Characteristics: Flexible, thrives on variety, energized by last-minute opportunities.

Effect on Goals –

Strengths: Adaptable and able to pivot quickly when challenges arise.

Challenges: May struggle with consistency and long-term planning.

Action Plan Tips:
- o Keep goals broad with flexible action steps.

o Use daily or weekly checklists to ensure progress without stifling spontaneity.
o Pair with a structured partner or accountability system for balance.

Organized Work Style

Characteristics: Methodical, focused, values routines and predictability.
Effect on Goals –
    Strengths: Excellent at implementing systems and maintaining consistency.
    Challenges: May struggle with adapting to unexpected changes or uncertainty.
Action Plan Tips:
o Create a detailed, step-by-step plan with contingency options.
o Use calendars and trackers to maintain a steady progress.
o Practice flexibility by setting aside time for unplanned tasks.

Innovative Work Style

Characteristics: Experimental, thrives on new ideas, challenges the status quo.
Effect on Goals –
    Strengths: Excels at thinking outside the box and finding unique solutions.
    Challenges: May lose focus or struggle with follow-through on repetitive tasks.
Action Plan Tips:
o Focus on one or two innovative ideas and break them into actionable steps.

- Partner with someone detail-oriented to ensure accountability.
- Use creativity-driven tools like mind maps or brainstorming apps.

Embrace Your Unique Blend of Work Styles

It's rare to fit perfectly into one work style category; most of us are a blend of several. Recognizing the traits that resonate most can help you craft a customized plan for success. Use the strengths that align with your goals and adjust strategies as needed to stay motivated. Your unique combination is your superpower—embrace it and adapt as circumstances or goals evolve. Flexibility and self-awareness are the keys to unleashing your potential!

Tailoring action plans to match work styles ensures a more personalized, effective approach to achieving goals. When you understand how your strengths and challenges play into your workflow, you're better equipped to succeed!

Work Style Discovery Questionnaire

This questionnaire will help you determine your primary work style and how much of a mix you might be. Answer the questions below honestly, selecting the option that best represents your typical behavior. Use the answer key and scoring instructions at the end to calculate your results.

Questions:
1. **When tackling a new project, your first instinct is to:**
   a. Dive in and figure things out as you go.
   b. Create a detailed plan and follow it step by step.

c. Collaborate with others to brainstorm ideas and solutions.

d. Research and gather as much information as possible before starting.

2. **How do you prefer to work in a team?**
   a. Take charge and guide the team toward a shared goal.
   b. Ensure everyone understands their roles and responsibilities.
   c. Act as the communicator, keeping the team connected and motivated.
   d. Focus on providing thorough analysis and insights.

3. **When facing a deadline you tend to:**
   a. Work intensively at the last minute to produce results.
   b. Stick to a pre-set schedule to stay on track.
   c. Seek input from others to ensure quality results.
   d. Double-check everything to ensure accuracy before submitting.

4. **What motivates you the most at work?**
   a. Achieving tangible results and recognition for your efforts.
   b. Meeting objectives efficiently and effectively.
   c. Building relationships and creating a positive environment.
   d. Learning, improving, and mastering skills.

5. **Your workspace is usually:**
   a. Dynamic and slightly chaotic, but you know where everything is.
   b. Organized, with everything in its place.
   c. Inviting, with personal touches to make it feel warm and friendly.
   d. Neat and functional, with a focus on efficiency.

6. **How do you handle unexpected challenges?**
    a. Adapt quickly and think on your feet.
    b. Revisit your plan and make necessary adjustments.
    c. Seek advice or input from trusted colleagues.
    d. Analyze the situation thoroughly before taking action.
7. **Success in your career means:**
    a. Reaching milestones and achieving significant goals.
    b. Maintaining a steady track record of reliable performance.
    c. Building strong relationships and a solid network.
    d. Gaining deep expertise and respect in your field.

Answer Key and Scoring:
- a = Dynamic/Action-Oriented
- b = Structured/Planner
- c = Collaborative/Relational
- d = Analytical/Thinker

Count how many of each letter you selected and calculate the percentage for each style: Percentage=(Count of Specific Letter/Total Number of Questions)

Example percentages would be:
 Dynamic/Action-Oriented = 3/7≈approx 43%
 Structured/Planner = 2/7≈approx 29%
 Collaborative/Relational = 17≈approx 14%
 Analytical/Thinker = 1/7≈approx 14%

Interpreting Results:
- Your highest percentage indicates your dominant work style.
- Use your mix to identify areas where blending strategies from other styles could benefit your goal-setting approach.

Example: If you are primarily Dynamic, integrate some structured elements to ensure long-term follow-through.

This personalized understanding will help you align your strengths with an action plan tailored to your unique work style blend!

Comprehensive Work Style Examples and Strategies

Below is a list of work styles, each paired with actionable approaches to help you align your unique traits with effective goal-setting and execution. You may notice that some styles—such as "Realist"—appear more than once. That's intentional. Certain traits naturally fit within multiple categories, and including them in each relevant group allows for deeper context and more tailored action steps. Each style is followed by practical strategies to make implementation straightforward and meaningful.

<u>Analytical Group</u>

Structured Thinker

- **Approach:** Use a detailed schedule with time-blocking and milestones.

- **Action:** Plan daily, weekly, and monthly tasks using a planner or app like Google Calendar or Asana. Outline your tasks clearly and ensure they fit into your overall timeline.

Detail-Oriented Worker

- **Approach:** Break large goals into micro-tasks.

- **Action:** Create a step-by-step checklist for each part of the goal to ensure no detail is overlooked. Use tools like Trello for organizing details.

Logical Thinker

- **Approach:** Use critical thinking to make strategic decisions.

- **Action:** Create pros and cons lists for major decisions and use data to guide your choices.

Analytical Thinker

- **Approach:** Use logic and data to make informed decisions.

- **Action:** Research and map out potential outcomes before acting to minimize risks.

Realist

- **Approach:** Identify practical steps and potential roadblocks.

- **Action:** Focus on tangible actions and create contingency plans to stay confident and prepared.

Creative Group

Big Picture Dreamer

- **Approach:** Focus on vision-driven outcomes.

- **Action:** Use vision boards or set broad milestones to maintain alignment with your larger vision.

Creative Thinker

- **Approach:** Use brainstorming and experimentation to discover solutions.

- **Action:** Dedicate time to free-thinking sessions and allow for trial-and-error learning.

Creatively Chaotic

- **Approach:** Harness creativity in a dynamic, unstructured way.

- **Action:** Keep a flexible list of priorities without rigid timelines and allow room for spontaneous ideas.

Big Goals Thinker

- **Approach:** Dream big and take bold steps.

- **Action:** Divide lofty goals into actionable phases with clear milestones to keep the dream manageable.

Independent Group

Self-Motivated

- **Approach:** Build intrinsic motivation through self-rewards.

- **Action:** Set personal incentives for completing milestones, such as treating yourself to something special after a major accomplishment.

Independent Worker

- **Approach:** Work autonomously to maximize productivity.

- **Action:** Set personal deadlines and goals, relying on self-discipline to drive progress.

Early Bird

- **Approach:** Use morning energy for focused work.

- **Action:** Schedule high-priority tasks for early hours and leave lighter work for later in the day.

Night Owl

- **Approach:** Capitalize on late-night productivity.
- **Action:** Plan deep work during the evening hours and use mornings for lighter or routine tasks.

Collaborative Group

Externally Motivated

- **Approach:** Leverage accountability partners or external deadlines.
- **Action:** Share your goals with a trusted partner who will check in regularly and provide encouragement.

People-Oriented

- **Approach:** Collaborate and connect for motivation.
- **Action:** Partner with others or join a group working toward similar goals for support and shared accountability.

Emotional Thinker

- **Approach:** Use passion and intuition to stay motivated.
- **Action:** Align goals with personal values and emotions, ensuring that your heart is fully invested in the process.

Team Player

- **Approach:** Collaborate for motivation and accountability.
- **Action:** Join a mastermind group or schedule regular check-ins with teammates to stay on track.

Pragmatic Group

Task-Oriented

- **Approach:** Focus on objectives and deadlines.
- **Action:** Prioritize a to-do list and work in uninterrupted time blocks to minimize distractions.

Realist

- **Approach:** Identify practical steps and potential roadblocks.
- **Action:** Focus on tangible actions and create contingency plans to stay confident and prepared.

Risk-Averse

- **Approach:** Build confidence through stable, predictable steps.
- **Action:** Start with small, low-risk actions to reduce stress and gain a sense of control.

Small Goals Thinker

- **Approach:** Focus on achievable, short-term wins.
- **Action:** Set incremental targets and celebrate small victories to maintain momentum.

Perfectionist

- **Approach:** Focus on progress over perfection.
- **Action:** Set "good enough" standards and establish strict time limits for tasks to prevent over-polishing.

Supportive Group

People-Oriented

- **Approach:** Collaborate and connect for motivation.

- **Action:** Partner with others or join a group working toward similar goals for support and shared accountability.

Team Player

- **Approach:** Collaborate for motivation and accountability.

- **Action:** Join a mastermind group or schedule regular check-ins with teammates to stay on track.

Emotional Thinker

- **Approach:** Use passion and intuition to stay motivated.

- **Action:** Align goals with personal values and emotions, ensuring that your heart is fully invested in the process.

Optimist

- **Approach:** Maintain positivity to drive ambition.

- **Action:** Use affirmations and visualization techniques to keep motivation high, even during tough moments.

Spontaneous Group

Flexible Thinker

- **Approach:** Embrace adaptability by setting broader goals.

- **Action:** Use task lists without strict deadlines; focus on completing key priorities by the end of the week or month.

Fast Starter

- **Approach:** Channel early momentum into quick wins.

- **Action:** Begin with simple, high-impact tasks to build confidence and gain traction.

Impulse-Driven

- **Approach:** Use bursts of energy to complete tasks quickly.

- **Action:** Focus on one goal at a time and channel impulsiveness effectively by prioritizing high-impact tasks.

Procrastinator

- **Approach:** Use urgency to focus energy.

- **Action:** Set hard deadlines or use countdown timers to create a sense of urgency and overcome delays.

Slow Starter

- **Approach:** Build momentum gradually by starting with low-pressure activities.

- **Action:** Set a timer for 10 minutes to begin a task without commitment to finish, easing into productivity.

Organized Group

Structured Thinker

- **Approach:** Use a detailed schedule with time-blocking and milestones.

- **Action:** Plan daily, weekly, and monthly tasks using a planner or app like Google Calendar or Asana. Outline your tasks clearly and ensure they fit into your overall timeline.

Task-Oriented

- **Approach:** Focus on objectives and deadlines.

- **Action:** Prioritize a to-do list and work in uninterrupted time blocks to minimize distractions.

Highly Organized

- **Approach:** Use detailed plans and checklists to maintain control.

- **Action:** Utilize tools like Trello, Asana, or a daily planner to track progress and ensure every step is accounted for.

Long-Term Planner

- **Approach:** Set multi-year goals and track milestones regularly.

- **Action:** Use goal-mapping tools to connect daily tasks to long-term outcomes, ensuring consistent progress over time.

Innovative Group

Big Picture Dreamer

- **Approach:** Focus on vision-driven outcomes.

- **Action:** Use vision boards or set broad milestones to maintain alignment with your larger vision.

Creative Thinker

- **Approach:** Use brainstorming and experimentation to discover solutions.

- **Action:** Dedicate time to free-thinking sessions and allow for trial-and-error learning.

Risk-Taker

- **Approach:** Take bold steps while planning contingencies.

- **Action:** Pursue high-reward opportunities while creating backup plans to minimize potential setbacks.

Innovative Thinker

- **Approach:** Use brainstorming and experimentation to discover solutions.

- **Action:** Dedicate time to free-thinking sessions and allow for trial-and-error learning.

Integrating Work Styles Into Your Journey

Each of these work styles highlights different approaches to goal setting and action planning. As you read through these, identify which ones resonate most with you. You may find that a mix of styles suits your needs depending on the goal or task at hand. Adjust strategies as needed, combining approaches to align with your strengths, minimize weaknesses, and stay motivated.

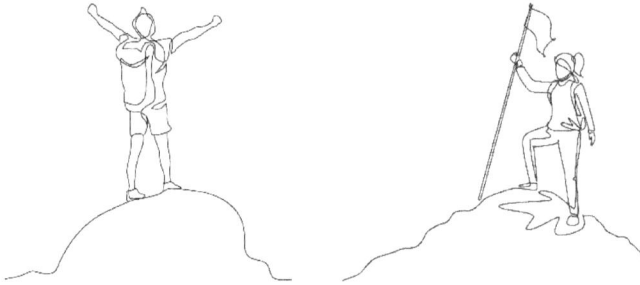

Closing: Embrace the Journey, Achieve the Goal

As we come to the end of this guide, remember: your journey is uniquely yours. It is as much about who you become along the way as it is about reaching the destination. The steps you've taken by reflecting on your goals, understanding your work style, and planning with intention are not just actions; they are investments in your growth, resilience, and ultimate success.

Bringing It All Together

The first part of this book set the foundation. You explored **The Destination**, where you clarified your goals and uncovered your "why." You learned about the importance of setting boundaries, selecting supportive travel partners, and embracing your strengths while growing through challenges. You prepared for the storms and obstacles with self-awareness, tools, and strategies to keep you moving forward, even when the road got rough.

The second part of this journey equipped you with actionable tools to build habits, routines, and strategies that align with your unique work style and strengths. Whether you're a structured thinker or creatively chaotic, a risk-taker or risk-averse, you now have the tools to tailor your journey to suit your natural tendencies while addressing areas of growth.

The Power of Reflection and Action

The process of combining clarity, action, and reflection has been central to this guide. Here's a recap to tie everything together:

1. **Define Your Goals:**
   Be clear, specific, and bold in declaring what you want to achieve. Revisit your "why" when motivation wanes. Keep your eyes on the prize, but also embrace the beauty of each step along the way.

2. **Build an Action Plan:**
   Use the SMART method to create achievable steps, and track your progress with tools that resonate with your work style. Your planner, action steps worksheet, and the intentional habits you've built are all tools for continued success.

3. **Embrace Flexibility:**
   Life happens. Storms come. But as you've learned,

flexibility is not a detour—it's an opportunity to grow and discover new paths. Stay adaptable, reassess when needed, and use your values as a compass.

4. **Celebrate Success:**
    Along the way, you've been encouraged to acknowledge each victory, no matter how small. Milestones are stepping stones to greater things. Reward yourself, reflect, and take pride in your achievements.

5. **Shine Your Light:**
    Embracing your journey isn't just about personal fulfillment. By growing, sharing, and supporting others, you contribute to a cycle of positivity that ripples outward. Your success inspires those around you, and their encouragement propels you further.

Bonus – Top Tips

There are a few steps we can take that really help move the needle. Think of it as your pre-flight checklist—your warm-up before diving into the real work. These are especially helpful when your goals feel big, bold, or just plain hard. You might've heard some of these before, but these are my personal, can't-skip, top "musts."

1. Clear the clutter (and not just the kind in your closet)

Sure, cleaning up your space at home or at work can help set the tone—and that's a big part of creating an environment that supports your goals. But the clutter I'm talking about here goes way deeper. I'm talking about the noise and nonsense that fills up our days.

Take a good look at what's entering your life on a daily basis. Then really ask: *What value is this bringing me?* Is it actually necessary? Or just something you've *always done?*

Let's talk TV for a sec. Years ago, during a tough season in my life, I realized that the news and all that background noise was just draining my energy. I asked myself—what am I really getting from this? Were the biased news segments helping me? Nope. Were the commercials giving me joy? Nope. Was watching the chaos of the world improving my daily life? Not one bit. And could I personally change any of it? Also nope.

So I shut it off. That was *my* clutter. (Not saying you shouldn't stay informed or make a difference—but for me, that wasn't the way.)

Now, let's talk social media. Are you using it as a tool? Or is it using you ? It's *amazing* for connecting with clients and building relationships. But let's be honest—we've all fallen down the scroll-hole and come out 30 minutes later with nothing to show for it.

What are the "have to's" filling up your day? Do they actually align with your goals and the life you want to build? Or are they just things you're doing because you feel like you *should?*

Only you can answer that. But it's worth digging into. Could be little things, could be big. Either way—take inventory.

Here's a fun example: I was raised to believe you *have* to balance your checkbook. Religiously. But these days? I haven't "balanced" a checkbook in years, and guess what? I'm fine! I keep an eye on deposits, glance at debits, and call it good. At year-end when I reconcile, I'm rarely off by more than a few cents—even in my business accounts. I adjust it and move on. Done.

2. Take one full day of real rest each week

This one's a game-changer, and it's about so much more than just getting enough sleep—though yes, that matters too! I'm talking about intentionally carving out *one day each week* where you lay the heavy stuff down. The decisions, the deadlines, the responsibilities—put them aside and shift your focus to what truly fills you up.

What excites you? What brings you joy? What makes you feel alive and rested? Whatever that is, do more of *that* on your day of rest.

And let me be clear—this isn't about jamming the day full of "fun" things and exhausting yourself in a new way. A day full of errands, sports, appointments, and social commitments doesn't count as rest just because it's not labeled "work." Rest means restoration. Refueling your soul. Reconnecting with your purpose. Letting your mind breathe.

This kind of rest includes quiet. It means shutting out the constant input and actually sitting with your thoughts. No background noise. No scrolling. Just you, your thoughts, your breath, your spirit. And yes—it might feel weird at first. We're so used to filling every second that silence can feel uncomfortable. But that stillness? That's where clarity lives.

And here's what's beautiful—when you start honoring one day of true rest each week, something incredible happens. You'll notice that your other six days get better. Stronger. More productive. More intentional.

You instinctively begin to put more focus and energy into your work because you *know* that one day break is coming. It creates rhythm. It brings balance. At first, it may feel a little stressful. You'll wonder, "How will I get everything done?" But over time, you'll actually find yourself getting more done in less time—and with more clarity.

You'll start to *look forward* to that day. It becomes a highlight of your week. A protected space for you to breathe, dream, rest, reflect. And when you step back into your week, you'll notice something else—you're energized. More creative. More focused. More excited for what's ahead.

Try it. One day. Each week. You're worth that.

3. Be mindful of what enters your space

You *get to choose* what comes into your life—your time, your energy, your headspace. What are you watching? What are you listening to? Are you afraid of missing out, so you let anything and everything in?

Evaluate the value. Is it worth it?

Then ask—who's in your circle? Are they building you up? Are you building them up? We were created to have an impact on others. That's a beautiful thing. But sometimes we need to step back and ask: *Is this relationship still good for both of us?* And if not? It's okay to release it.

I can hear the pushback already. "But it's family..." Yep. I get it. You may not be able to eliminate that relationship—but you *can* minimize the time spent, or shift how you show up in it. You can mentally and emotionally distance from the dysfunction. It takes practice. Trust me—I've had to do it, too.

Maybe your clutter is the newest tech gadget that's calling your name. The shiny distraction. But ask yourself—how does this serve your goals or your purpose? Is it helpful or just noise?

Spring clean your life. Take a good look at what's in your space—physically, mentally, emotionally. Not because anything or anyone is inherently "bad," but because *you* are refining your world for what matters most. For what actually moves you forward.

4. Be focused... but stay flexible

Focus is key to success. That's why tools like planners, vision boards, accountability partners, and good old task lists are so powerful. They help keep your eyes on the destination.

But—and this is a big one—don't get cemented into one idea of how the journey *has* to look.

Life throws curveballs. Detours pop up. Sometimes new opportunities show up that we never even imagined. Or a goal you once had starts evolving into something bigger—something better.

So yes, stay focused. But stay open. Don't let your own expectations box you in.

Ask yourself—Is there a smarter way to do this? Could this evolve into something new? Can I pivot? Should I outsource? Is the person I hired for admin work actually a rockstar in marketing?

Stay curious. Stay teachable. Stay flexible.

These steps may feel simple—but don't underestimate how powerful they can be when you actually walk them out. You don't need perfection. You just need progress. Keep refining. Keep moving. You've got this.

Your Journey Is Ongoing

This book has given you tools to start or refine your journey, but it's just the beginning. Goals evolve, challenges arise, and opportunities will appear. Each new chapter is an invitation to grow, stretch, and strive toward your best self. Remember, no obstacle can stop your progress except the decision to stop moving forward.

Your Final Action Plan

Take a moment now to create your action plan. Here are a few prompts to guide you:

- **Revisit Your Goals:** What is your primary goal right now? Are your actions aligned with your purpose?

- **Evaluate Your Progress:** Which strategies and tools have worked best for you so far? What adjustments do you need to make?

- **Check Your Compass:** Are you staying true to your values? Do your choices reflect the person you want to become?

- **Renew Your Motivation:** What excites you most about your journey? How can you keep that energy alive?

- **Contribute to Others' Journeys:** How can you lend your experience and light to someone else who is striving toward their own destination?

Write these answers in your planner, notebook, or on your digital app. They will be your guideposts as you move forward.

Be Brave. Be Unstoppable.

You've got this. The road ahead may twist and turn, but every experience—every step—is part of the adventure. Embrace the journey, knowing that it is shaping you into the person you are meant to be.

So, what's your next step? Take it with courage, determination, and the unshakable belief that you are capable of achieving anything. The world is waiting for you to shine. **Go forth and conquer!**

■ Author's Note

This book was born from lived experience—hard-won, deeply felt, and constantly evolving.

Embrace the Journey is more than a title—it's a philosophy I've learned (and re-learned) through successes, setbacks, and seasons that didn't make sense at the time. I've failed forward, held on to faith when the road got steep, and discovered that the most meaningful growth often comes from the hardest places. If you find yourself questioning your worth, stuck between chapters, or trying to push past inner or outer anchor points—you're not alone. This book is for you.

I didn't write this because I have all the answers. I wrote it because I've asked all the questions. And because I believe with everything in me that your journey matters. It's sacred ground—even the messy parts.

As you turn these pages, my hope is that you feel seen, encouraged, and reminded of your own strength. Growth doesn't mean becoming someone else—it means returning to who you truly are, one brave step at a time.

We may not always get to choose the terrain, but we can choose how we show up for the journey.

With grit, grace, and hope,
Jenny Carlson

◼ About the Author

Jenny Carlson is a writer, entrepreneur, educator, and real estate professional whose passion lies in helping others grow with purpose. For more than two decades, she has taught personal and professional development through a lens of authenticity, faith, and forward movement.

Before launching a career in real estate, Jenny worked as a small business consultant and facilitator, guiding others toward meaningful success. She is the founder of **StreamLine Agents, Inc.,** a transaction coordination firm, and **StreamLine Marketing Pro,** a platform designed to empower real estate agents with strategic branding and automation tools. In every role she plays—teacher, mentor, business owner, or friend—her greatest mission is to help others navigate the path toward wholeness and impact.

Jenny lives in Texas, where her love for freedom, faith, and nature runs deep. She shares her days with a beloved collection of animals, among them three goats (Hansel, Gretel, and Balky) and their loyal guardian dog, Cotton. Her heart beats for natural healing, the wisdom of creation, and meaningful connection with the people in her life.

Embrace the Journey is her first book, but it is far from the beginning of her story.

To connect, explore resources, or learn more, visit: www.embrace-the-journey.org

✦ Let's Keep the Journey Going

If *Embrace the Journey* encouraged you, challenged you, or helped you find clarity along the way, I would be so grateful if you'd take a moment to leave a review.

Your words help others discover the book—and maybe find what they need, too.

Leave a review on Amazon or Goodreads. It truly makes a difference.

✦ More for the Journey

▥ Grab the Embrace the Journey Planner

Designed to help you take your next steps with purpose and clarity. Available on www.embrace-the-journey.org

▤ Companion Journal (Coming Soon!)

A guided space to reflect, reset, and keep moving forward.

⌨ Visit the Website

Get updates, download resources, and access free tools: www.embrace-the-journey.org

▤ Join the Community on Facebook

Let's connect, grow, and support one another.
Search: *Embrace the Journey with Jenny Carlson*

❤ With gratitude—thank you for being part of this journey.

You are seen. You are capable. You are never alone.

www.ingramcontent.com/pod-product-compliance
Lightning Source LLC
LaVergne TN
LVHW051240080426
835513LV00016B/1688